THE HYMNS AND HYMN TUNES
FOUND IN THE
ENGLISH METRICAL PSALTERS

THE HYMNS

Found in the

COLEMAN-ROSS COMPANY, INC.

AND HYMN TUNES

English

Metrical Psalters

By EDNA PARKS

NEW YORK • NINETEEN SIXTY-SIX

DEDICATED TO MY MOTHER

PREFACE

NEARLY ALL WRITERS CONCERNED WITH CONGREGA-
TIONAL SINGING IN ENGLAND at the time of the Reforma-
tion have directed their attention to the use of metrical versions of the
Psalms and often tell us that no other kind of religious verse was
acceptable in the church service at that time. Nevertheless, by the mid-
sixteenth century there were freely composed hymns being written in
English for use in the English church. It has been my purpose to
present here the six hymns found in the early Sternhold and Hopkins
Psalters, along with a study of their tunes. The six hymns are traced
through succeeding Psalters from c. 1560 to the end of the eighteenth
century. Since they were used in the church service at the time of the
Reformation, these hymns share with the metered Psalms the distinction of establishing in England the practice of congregational singing
in the language of the people. The harmonizations of the tunes, as they
are followed from the time of the Reformation through the next two
centuries, faithfully reflect, in their miniature way, characteristic vocal
writing of English composers of the various periods.

My work in this field began during graduate study at Boston
University and the material presented here is a revision of part of a
doctoral dissertation submitted to that University with additional information gathered since that time. I am indebted to Dr. Otto Kinkledey
for the suggestion that such a study was needed and for his interest and

help in the work. I am grateful, also, to Dr. Karl Geiringer and Professor John Hasson at Boston University and Professor Harry E. Bell at Oxford University for counsel and advice which aided me in locating valuable information. Dr. Gustave Reese very kindly read the complete typescript and gave helpful criticism and comments.

The hymns in Chapter II are taken from a very rare volume of Psalters found at the Boston Public Library in a collection of early Psalters and Books of Common Prayer made available to the Library through the beneficence of Josiah H. Benton. The photographic reproductions from the volume were provided by courtesy of the Trustees of the Boston Public Library.

I remember with gratitude the many courtesies extended to me at Union Theological Seminary Library, the British Museum, the Bodleian Library, Christ Church Library, the Royal School of Music, the Henry E. Huntington Library, and Houghton Library at Harvard University. Mr. John Alden, the Keeper of the Rare Books at the Boston Public Library, provided unfailingly cheerful help in my work there.

A Danforth Foundation grant from Wheaton College, Norton, Massachusetts helped to make possible the work done in England.

EDNA PARKS

Method Used for Transcription
of Tunes and Hymns

All of the tunes are placed on treble and/or bass staff and kept in the same register as the original. The original clef and staff are shown at the beginning of each example. The semibreve is made to equal a whole-note; the minim, a half-note, etc. The long and the breve at the ends of phrases or final cadences are transcribed as whole-notes with fermatas. Accidental signs in parentheses above the staff do not appear in the original music.

The meter and rhyme scheme of the hymns are shown in the example which presents a hymn for the first time. Then follows the author of the publication, title of publication, date, and pages where music was found, if pages were numbered. A *Short Title Catalogue* number is added where possible.

The texts were not divided into syllables in the Psalters, and where it was necessary to sing more than one note to a syllable there was no indication about the number of notes to use. The division into syllables has been made in the reproductions by this writer to aid the reader, and the text underlaying in the ambiguous spots is presented as a singable solution but is not intended to eliminate speculation about the "correct" placing of the words. The original spelling with all its inconsistencies has been retained as a means of identification among editions.

ABBREVIATIONS

C.M.	Common Meter
C.M.D.	Common Meter Double
L.M.	Long Meter
L.M.D.	Long Meter Double
S.T.C.	*Short Title Catalogue 1475-1640*

Metrical schemes of the verse, in addition to those listed above, are shown in the usual way, e.g., 6.6.6.6.6.6. indicates six lines, each with six syllables.

The scheme of the rhyme is shown with letters, e.g., *abab* indicates four lines with first and third lines rhyming, and second and fourth lines rhyming.

CONTENTS

Authority for Congregational Hymn Singing

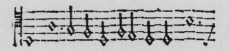

The first parte

of the Booke of Psalmes, collected into English Metre, by
Thomas Sternehold, Ihon Hopkins
and others : conferred with the
Hebrue, with apte notes to singe
them withall.

Newly set forth and allowed to be song
in Churches, of al the people together,
before and after Mornyng and Euening
Prayer, as also before and after the Sermons and moreouer in priuate houses, for their
godly solace and comfort, laying apart all vn
godlye songes and balades, whiche tende
onely to the nourishyng of vice, and
corrupting of youth.
Wherunto is added the Cathechisme for children, and also a short introduction to
learne to sing these Psalmes.

IAMES 5.

If any be afflicted, let him pray, and if any
be mery, let him sing Psalmes.

COLLOS. 3.

Let the worde of God dwel plenteouslye in all
wisdom, teaching and exhorting one an other in
Psalmes, Hymnes, and spiritual songes,
and sing vnto the Lord in your harts.

Imprinted at London by Ihon Daye.

Cum priuilegio Regiæ Maiestatis
per Decennium.
Forbidding all other to printe these
Psalmes or any part of them.

Title page *The first parte of the Booke of Psalmes* (1569)

CHAPTER I

NE OF THE FIRST outward signs that the Reformation had been accomplished was the use of congregational singing in the vernacular. The kind of composition used for this purpose varied within the different branches of Protestantism, and in England the people of the parish churches were singing canticles, hymns,[1] and metrical Psalms in English by the mid-sixteenth century.

The long history of the Christian hymn is well known. Matthew and Mark mention that a hymn was sung at the close of the Last Supper. Both St. Hilary and St. Ambrose wrote hymns, and in spite of some opposition to their use, a place was made for them in the Offices. By the middle of the twelfth century in England, both the secular clergy and the monastic clergy had introduced hymns into the service, but these were all Latin hymns and were sung only by clergy and choir, usually in procession before and after Mass, or as Office hymns. Hymns in the vernacular for congregational use appeared with the Reformation, just

---

[1] A hymn in this study is to be distinguished from a Psalm in metrical form. It is simple, original poetry without specific scriptural basis. It is suitable for congregational singing when joined with a tune, and it expresses either God's purpose in the life of man or man's praise or prayer to God. See "What is a Hymn?" by Carl F. Price, *The Papers of The Hymn Society*, VI, 1937.

as they had in Bohemia where a Hussite hymnal was published in 1501, and in Germany where Luther introduced hymn singing in the reorganized church service of the early sixteenth century.

The Reformation came later in England than on the Continent. It was the parliament assembled in 1529 by Henry VIII that ended the control of the church by the pope, but few doctrinal changes were made at that time. These came rapidly under the strong Protestant direction of the Duke of Somerset and the regency council governing for Edward VI, so that by 1553, when Mary Tudor became Queen, Archbishop Cranmer's Prayer Book in English was already in use. Thereupon followed a brief period when Roman ritual was restored, but at the beginning of Elizabeth's reign in 1558, Protestantism was reinstated, this time with some degree of stability. It was at this time, too, that hymns of free poetic invention in the vernacular came into use in the service, joined with the English metrical versions of the canticles and Psalms.

When Elizabeth again established the Prayer Book after five years of Roman supremacy, she did not share the Protestant dislike for elaborate music and organ playing. Warton tells how the English who had fled to Geneva during Mary's reign now returned and waged vigorous attack against the solemn ceremonies of the English church service, in an attempt to inaugurate the austere form of worship of Calvinism.[1] Had they been successful, service music would have been limited to unaccompanied, unison, congregational singing with the added requirement that all texts used could be found in the Bible, primarily in the Psalms. Elizabeth and her bishops were not persuaded to change the service and Item 49 of *Injunctions Given by the Queen's Majesty concerning both the clergy and laity of this Realm Published Anno Dom. 1559* made this very clear.

> 49. Item, because in divers Collegiate, and also some Parish Churches heretofore there have been livings appointed for the maintenance of men and children to use singing in the Church by means whereof the laudable service of Musick hath been had in estimation and preserved in knowledge: the Queen's Majesty neither meaning in any wise the decay of any thing that might conveniently tend to the use and continuance of the said Science, neither to have the same in any part so abused in the church, that thereby the Common Prayer should

1 Thomas Warton, *The History of English Poetry*, London, 1870, p. 741.

be the worse understanded of the hearers, willeth and commandeth, that first no alterations be made of such arrangements of living, as heretofore hath been appt. to the use of singing or musicke in the Church, but that the same so remain, And that there be a modest and distinct song so used in all parts of the Common prayers in the church, that the same may be as plainly understanded, as if it were read without singing, and yet nevertheless, for the comforting of such as delight in musick, it may be permitted, that in the beginning or in the end of Common prayer, either at morning or evening, there may be sung an hymn, or such like song, to the praise of Almighty God, in the best sort of melody and musick that may be conveniently devised, having in respect that the sentence of the Hymn may be understanded and perceived.[1]

It is difficult to tell what kind of composition was meant by *hymn* in this passage. Paul Henry Lang in his *Music in Western Civilization* interprets the "hymn or such like song" to mean anthem. The "such like song" may very well have been an anthem but it is not unreasonable to assume that *hymn* referred to freely composed religious verse to be sung by the congregation, for immediately after the Injunctions in 1559, compositions of this kind began to appear in the Psalters, with direction for their use at stated points in the service. These were original hymns, not anthems, nor metered Psalms, nor canticles, and their appearance so soon after the Injunctions would seem to indicate that they had been in use before the authorization, awaiting only this official approval before being printed.

To be sure, the first attempt to write hymns in English had been made before this time. Myles Coverdale was the author of *Goostly Psalmes and Spiritual Songs,* a volume with chorale-like tunes, published soon after 1529. Except for the first and last hymns, all were translations from the German or Latin and kindled little interest among the English people.[2] The time was not yet ripe for the appearance of the indigenous English hymn; the Reformation was not far enough advanced.

There were other metrical Psalters between the time of Coverdale's

---

[1] *Injunctions Given by the Queen's Majesty concerning both the clergy and laity of this Realm,* London, 1559, p. 75.

[2] The banning of the Coverdale book by Henry VIII in 1539 does not seem to me to be sufficient reason for the neglect of the hymns. If the people had been genuinely interested in them, the verses would have found their way into use.

book and 1547 when the first of the long series of Sternhold's came out, but as far as is known, there were no hymns in the collections. Nor did Thomas Sternhold, Psalm-singing groom of robes to Henry VIII and Edward VI, include any in his first little volume. There were none in the edition of 1549 which presented all of the Psalms that Sternhold had versified before his death in August of that year, along with seven by John Hopkins, later rector of Great Waldingfield, Suffolk. In the same year, 1549, Robert Crowley published a complete Psalter in common meter with what is believed to be the earliest extant music for the English metrical Psalm. Here we find added to the Psalms, the Magnificat, Nunc Dimittis, Benedictus, Song of Three Children, Te Deum, and Creed of Athanasius; all in verse, but still no hymns. Perhaps as early as 1559 and certainly not later than 1562, six poems were inserted in the sections of canticles preceding and following the main body of Psalms in the Sternhold and Hopkins collections. These six poems expressed prayer and praise to God. The verses were apparently conceived in English and were intended to be sung. Together they share the distinction of being the first English hymns for use in the church service. The titles and first lines of the six were:

The Lamentation of a sinner, "O Lord turne not away thy face"
The prayer vnto the holy ghost, "Come holy sprite the God of might"
The complaint of a sinner, "Where righteousness doth say"
A thankesgeuing after the receiuing of the Lordes supper, "The Lord
    be thanked for his giftes"
A Lamentation, "O Lord in thee is all my trust"
The Humble Sute of the Sinner, "O Lord of whō I do depend"

The First Six Hymns
and Their Tunes

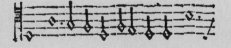

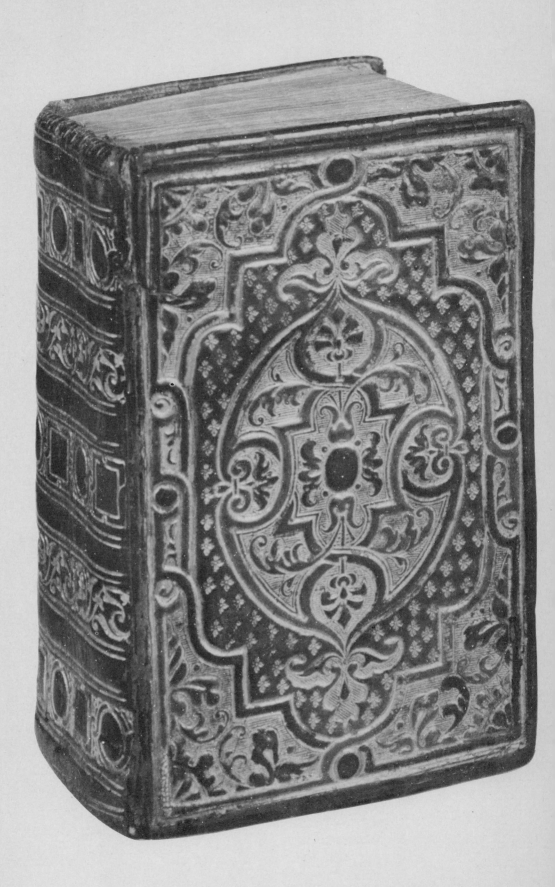

CHAPTER II

THE SIX HYMNS and their tunes are reproduced here as they are found in a beautifully bound volume in the Benton Collection at the Boston Public Library. Five of them are in a Sternhold and Hopkins Psalter and the sixth one is in a Hopkins Psalter, both books being bound together, along with a Book of Common Prayer, a prose Psalter, and the Epistles and Gospels.[1] It is interesting to speculate about the date of publication of the Sternhold and Hopkins called *The first parte of the Booke of Psalmes,* as no date appears on the title page. There is a colophon with the date 1569, but attached to the back cover is page seventy-one of a book dealer's catalogue, identified in a handwritten note as Ellis and Elvey, 1896, and another MS note in the margin states that the 1569 date is a misprint for 1559. To substantiate the early date, attention is drawn to the Hopkins Psalter bound with the Sternhold. The publication date of the Hopkins Psalter, presumably the only one published by Hopkins alone, is 1562 and its purpose was to provide anyone who already owned a Psalter with another one which, when joined with the first, would furnish the singer with the complete 150 Psalms. Study of the two volumes here bound together shows that the

---

[1] See Appendix for description of the volume; photograph on page 6.

purpose of the Hopkins book was accomplished if used with this edition of the Sternhold called "first parte," for all of the Psalms not in it are in the Hopkins, along with seven duplications; these seven using a different versification from the versions in the Sternhold.[1]

Leaving speculation aside, however, the *Lamentation,* "O Lord in thee is all my trust" was published by Day in *Certaine notes set forth in foure and three parts to be song at the Morning Communion, and euening praier* in 1560. "O Lord turn not away thy face," "Come, holy sprite," and "The Lord be thanked" were included in the 1561 Sternhold Psalter.[2] "O Lord of whom I do depend," "Where righteousness doth say," and the other four which had appeared earlier were all in the Sternhold and Hopkins *The Whole Booke of Psalmes,* 1562.

The hymns are reproduced here in the order in which they were printed in the Sternhold "first parte." Markant, to whom the *Lamentation of a sinner* was attributed, was rector of Great Clacton in the second year of Elizabeth's reign.

Example 1.

The Lamentation of a sinner
"O Lord turne not away thy face"
[First publication 1561]
C.M.D.
abcbdefe

Thomas Sternehold and Jhon Hopkins, *The first parte of the Booke of Psalmes,* 1569, pp. 19-21.

1st line   2nd line   succeeding lines*

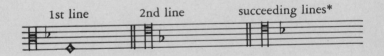

* In the original the clef and the flat were not correctly placed until the third line.

Markant

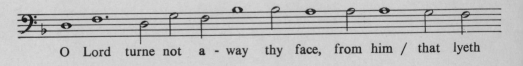

O Lord turne not a - way thy face, from him / that lyeth

---

[1] See Appendix for a copy of the title page, table of contents, and further discussion of the publication date of the Hopkins Psalter.

[2] Maurice Frost, *English and Scottish Psalm and Hymn Tunes c. 1543-1677,* London, 1953, p. 12.

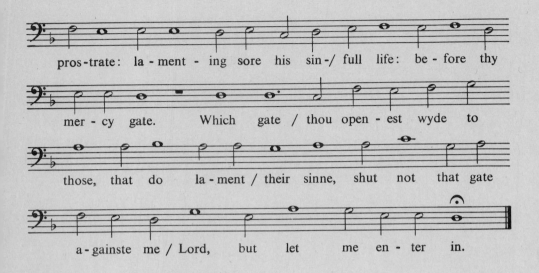

pros-trate: la-ment-ing sore his sin-/ full life: be-fore thy
mer-cy gate. Which gate / thou open-est wyde to
those, that do la-ment / their sinne, shut not that gate
a-gainste me / Lord, but let me en-ter in.

THE LAMENTATION OF A SINNER
John Markant

O Lord turne not away thy face,
    From him that lyeth prostrate:
Lamenting sore his sinfull life:
    Before thy mercy gate.
Which gate thou openest wyde to those,
    That do lament their sinne,
Shut not that gate againste me Lord,
    But let me enter in.

    And call me not to mine accompts,
How I have liued here:
For then I know right well O Lord,
How vile I shall appeare.
    I nede not to confesse my life,
I am sure thou canst tell:
What I have bene, and what I am,
I know thou knowest it well.

    O Lord thou knowest what thinges be past,
And eke the things that be:
Thou knowest also what is to come,
Nothing is hid from thee.

Before the heauens and earth were made,
Thou knowest what thinges were then:
As all thinges els that hath bene since
Among the sonnes of men.

And can the thinges that I haue done,
Be hidden from thee then?
Nay, nay, thou knowest them all O Lord,
Where they were done and when.
Wherefore with teares I come to thee,
To beg and to entreate:
Euen as the childe that hath done euill,
And feareth to be beat.

So come I to thy mercy gate,
Where mercy doth abound:
Requiring mercy for my sinnes,
To heale my deadly wound.
O Lord I nede not to repeate,
What I do beg or craue:
Thou knowest O Lord before I aske,
The thing that I would haue.

Mercy good Lord mercy I aske,
This is the totall summe:
For mercy Lord is all my sute,
Lord let thy mercy come. Amen.

The tune is simple and expressive. The setting of the words is syllabic, in keeping with the reformers' efforts to simplify the service music, and providing for ease in congregational singing. The mode is Dorian with the flat used as signature because all of the B's would of necessity have to be lowered.[1] The ascending and descending movement in the melody is beautifully balanced and smoothly achieved with pre-

---

[1] Frere was mistaken, I think, when he wrote in his Introduction to the Historical Edition of *Hymns Ancient and Modern* that none of these six tunes was modal. It must be remembered that while the major/minor tonal system was evolving from the ecclesiastical modes, there was a period when a melody might already seem tonal. However, examination of a harmonization of such a tune, made by a musician contemporary with it, might very well show that he still heard the melody within the modal system.

dominantly stepwise progressions. The ascent is gradual to the highest point which is reached in the last line; the descent to the final more rapid, using three of the six leaps of a fourth found in the entire melody. There are eight phrases. Each one is different melodically but unity is successfully accomplished through repetition of rhythmic patterns. The pattern of the first phrase appears again in the fifth phrase with the sixth note changed from a whole-note to a half-note. This simple alteration eliminates a parallel construction and helps to make the little melody something more than a commonplace tune. The rhythmic pattern of the second phrase is repeated in the fourth phrase, with slight alteration in the sixth, and like the original again in the final phrase. The rhythm of the third phrase is found also in the seventh.

The composer of the tune is not known. Wooldridge thinks that Ravenscroft was probably right in saying that all of the Psalm tunes were "English tunes imitating the High Dutch, Italian, French and Netherlandish tunes."[1] He believes that there were many English musicians capable of writing them and no doubt some were found among the organists and singing men who fled to Geneva along with the clergy when Mary restored the Roman rites. Many of the tunes are found first in the Psalter printed at Geneva for use by the English and later came into England when the refugees returned. As far as is known, however, this tune for the *Lamentation* makes its first appearance with the hymn in 1561. It has none of the over-sweet sentimentality of the late eighteenth-century tunes. It is straightforward, easy to sing, and the free-flowing rhythm gives it a beauty that is not found in the tune *St. Mary* with which the hymn is associated in present-day books. One wishes that the original tune might be restored.

A prayer vnto the holy ghost, to be song before the sermon, is the second freely composed hymn found in the Sternhold and Hopkins "first parte."

[1] H. E. Wooldridge, "Psalter," *Grove's Dictionary,* 3rd ed., IV, 270. Revised by T.C.L. Pritchard in 5th ed.

Example 2.

A prayer vnto the holy ghost
"Come holy sprite the God of might"
[First publication 1561]
C.M.D.
abcbdefe
Thomas Sternehold and Jhon Hopkins, *The first parte of the Booke of Psalmes*, 1569, unpaged section.
Tune, *Psalm LXIX*, p. CXXXIX.

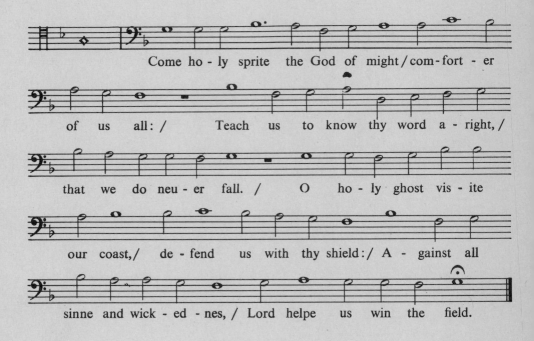

A PRAYER VNTO THE HOLY GHOST,
TO BE SONG BEFORE THE SERMON.
Sing this as the LXIX Psalme.

Come holy sprite the God of might
   comforter of us all:
Teach us to know thy word aright,
   that we do neuer fall.
O holy ghost visite our coast,
   defend us with thy shield:
Against all sinne and wickednes,
   Lorde helpe vs win the field.

Lord keepe our Queene and her Counsaile,
    and geue them will and might:
To perseuer in thy Gospell,
    which can put sinne to flight.
O Lorde that geuest thy holy word,
    send preachers plenteously:
That in the same we may accord,
    and therein liue and die.

O holy sprite direct aright,
    the preachers of thy word:
That thou by them maist cut downe sinne,
    as it were with a sword.
Depart not from those pastors pure,
    but ayde them at all neede:
Which breake to us the bread of life,
    whereon our soules do feed.

O blessed sprite of truth keepe us,
    in peace and unity:
Keepe us from sectes and errours all,
    and from all papistry.
Conuert all those that are our foes,
    and bring them to the light:
That they and we may well agree,
    and praise the day and night.

O Lord increase our faith in vs,
    and loue so to abound:
That man and wife be vyod of strife,
    and neighbours about vs round.
In our time geue thy peace (O Lord)
    to nations farr and nie:
And teach them all thy holy word,
    that we may sing to thee.

All glory to the Trinity,
    that is of mightes most,
The liuing father and the Sonne,
    and eke the holy ghost.
As it hath bene in all the time,
    that hath bene heretofore:
As it is now and so shalbe,
    henceforth for euermore.

The tune, in the second mode transposed, is a small two-part form with the second part a repetition of the first although not exact. There is an effect of modulation to what we now call F major at the end of the second and sixth phrases. A combination of madol and major/minor writing is common at this period, so close to the time when the major/minor tonality emerged from the ecclesiastical modes and became the accepted system. The interest in the hymn, however, lies not in the tune but rather in its use, for we find it mentioned by name in Cause Papers of the mid-sixteenth century.

The *Tudor Parish Documents of the Diocese of York* record the case against Melchior Smyth, Vicar of Hessle and Hull, in 1563/64. The complaint was made that

> Melchior making many sermons in the Trynitie churche of Hull in tyme of his first being resident there did always omytt and neglect to pray for the Quenes majestie. . . .[1]

In answer to the charge Melchior Smyth wrote

> He belevithe that at his first commyng to Hull he did use to make a generall praier for the churche the Quene and all other estates, after, for brevitie onelie and to avoyde tediousness he appoynted the hympne [sic] to be song called Come Holie Spiritt, at the begynnyng of everie sermon, Wherein the Quene, and her Counsell the Nobilitie the States bothe of the spiritualtie and temporaltie were praied for.[2]

The Reverend Melchior Smyth was also in trouble because in the "common Scholes" he was teaching the children of some of his friends "David's Psalmes and Calvyn's Cathechisme" in verse, and this offended the papists.[3]

There are several points of interest in this account of the case against Melchior Smyth. First of all, there was a church in Hull where a hymn was being sung regularly in the service as early as 1563. That it was a hymn and thought of as such by Mr. Smyth is shown by his use of the word in his defense against the charges made by his parishioners. He does not use hymn when he writes of other parts of the metered Psalter, such as "David's Psalmes and Calvyn's Cathechisme" in verse.

---

[1] *Tudor Parish Documents of the Diocese of York*, J. S. Purvis, Cambridge University Press, 1948, p. 212. "Articles and Answers in a cause, the Ecclesiastical Commissioners of York against Melchior Smith, Vicar of Hessle and Hull A.D. 1563/64." Cause Papers R-VII-G-1396.

[2] *Ibid.*, p. 217.

[3] *Ibid.*, p. 216.

Furthermore, he was using the hymn in the place in the service which was proper for it according to the instructions in the Psalter: before the sermon. As the sermon would probably follow either morning or evening prayer, the insertion of a hymn at this point was acknowledged by the Queen's Injunctions as an acceptable place for it. Apparently there was no objection from his parishioners because a hymn was sung; the complaint was concerned with what they believed to be the omission of a prayer for the Queen.

Added evidence that the hymn was acceptable and in use for many years thereafter is the change in the first line of stanza two from "Lorde-keepe our Queene and her Counsaile" to "Lorde keepe the king and his councell" in later editions of Psalters.

The third hymn in the Sternhold and Hopkins of 1569 is *The complaint of a sinner*, with the first line "Where righteousness doth say."

Example 3.

The complaint of a sinner
"Where righteousness doth say"
[First publication 1562]
6.6.6.6.6.6.6.6.6.
ababcdcdd
Thomas Sternehold and Jhon Hopkins, *The first parte of the Booke of Psalmes*, 1569. unpaged section.

THE COMPLAINT OF A SINNER

Where righteousness doth say;
Lord for my sinnefull part,
In wrath thou shouldst me pay,
Vengeance for my desert,
I can not it deny,
But needes I must confesse,
How that continually,
Thy laws I do transgresse.

But if it be thy will,
With sinners to contend:
Then all thy flocke shall spill,
And be lost without end.
For who liueth here so right,
That rightly he can say:
He sinneth not in thy sight,
Full often euery day.

The scripture plaine telleth me,
The righteous man offendeth:
Seuen times a day to thee,
Wheron thy wrath dependeth.
So that the righteous man,
Doth walke in no such path,
But he falleth now or than,
In daunger of thy wrath.

Then sith the case so standes,
That euen the man rightwise:
Falleth oft in sinfull handes,
Whereby thy wrath may rise.
Lord, I that am uniust,
And righteousnes none haues
Whereto then shall I trust,
My sinfull soule to saue?

But truely to that post,
Whereto I cleaue and shall:
Which is thy mercy most,
Lord let thy mercy fall.

And mitigate thy moode,
Or els we perish all:
The price of this thy bloud,
Wherin mercy I call.

Thy scripture doth declare,
No drop of bloud in thee:
But that thou didst not spare,
To shed ech drop for me.
Now let those drops most sweete,
So moist my hart so dry:
That I with sinne replete,
May liue and sinne may die.

That beyng mortified,
This sinne of mine in me:
I may be sanctified
By grace of thine in thee.
So that I neuer fall,
Into such mortall sinne:
That my foes infernall,
Reioyce my death therein.
But vouchsafe me to keepe,
From those infernall foes:
And from that lake so deepe,
Whereas no mercy growes.
And I shall sing the songes,
Confirmed with the iust:
That unto thee belonges,
Which art mine onely trust.

Neither hymn nor tune here is noteworthy. The verse is sheer doggerel. The mode of the tune is Dorian and the last note being the major third above the final is quite unexpected; 7-8 or 2-1 being the usual cadence. In addition, the last part of the tune, beginning at the words "I can it not deny," sounds to the modern ear like a modulation to F major moving into C major before the very abrupt return to the original mode. The three phrases beginning on C in this second part of the tune seem to lose momentum as the third one is unable to rise above the second. The first part of the tune is constructed in a small *abac* pattern and uses the device of musical rhyme.

The fourth hymn in the Psalter, *A thankesgeuing after the re-ceiuing of the Lordes supper,* is not given a separate tune, and the directions are to sing it to the tune of Psalm CXXXVII. The 124 lines of the poem are not divided into stanzas on the pages where they are printed except for indentation of every fourth line. The tune shows it to be in Common Double Meter. The great length of the hymn was no doubt due to its function in the service and could be used while a sizable number of communicants were served.

Example 4.
A thankesgeuing after the receiuing of the Lordes supper
"The Lord be thanked for his giftes"
[First publication 1561]
C.M.D.
abcbdefe
Thomas Sternehold and Jhon Hopkins, *The first parte of the Booke of Psalmes,* 1569, unpaged section.
Tune, *Psalm CXXXVII,* p. CXXVI.

[The last two notes, printed B and A in the Psalter, obviously should be D and C.]

A THANKESGEUING AFTER THE RECEIUING
OF THE LORDES SUPPER
Sing this as the CXXXVII Psalme.

The Lord be thanked for his giftes,
　　and mercy euermore:
That he doth shew vnto his saintes,
　　to him be laud therefore.
Our tonges cannot so praise the Lord,
　　as he doth right deserue:
Our hartes cannot of him so thinke,
　　as he doth vs preserue.

　　His benefites they be so great,
To vs that be but sinne:
That at our handes for recompence,
There is no hope to winne.
　　O sinfull fleshe that thou shouldst haue:
Such mercies of the Lord:
Thou doost deserue more worthely,
Of him to be abhord.
. . . .
　　Not one of vs that seeketh out,
The Lord of life to please:
Nor do the thing that might vs joyne
Our Christ and quiet ease.
　　Thus we are all his enemyes,
We can it not deny:
And he againe of his good will,
Would not that we should die.
. . . .
　　And as the cornes by unity,
Into one loafe is knit:
So is the Lord and his whole church
Though he in heauen sit.
　　As many grapes make but one wine
So should we be but one:
In faith and loue, in Christ aboue,
And vnto Christ alone.
. . . .

The tune is within the range of the Hypoionian mode and sounds

like our major mode. The entire melody entwines itself around the
notes of a triad built on the final. The last five notes of the first phrase
become the entire fourth phrase and then are used again in fragment
at the beginning of the fifth. The last phrase closely resembles the
second. In spite of the rather monotonous insistence on C, E, G, there
is a quality of humble dignity here quite suitable for the words of the
hymn.

Example 5.

A Lamentation
"O Lord in thee is all my trust"
[First publication 1560]
L.M.D.
ababcdcd
Thomas Sternehold and Jhon Hopkins, *The first parte of the
Booke of Psalmes*, 1569, unpaged section.

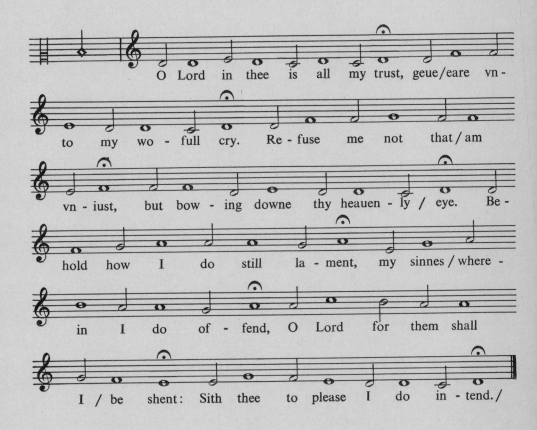

A LAMENTATION

O Lord in thee is all my trust,
    geue eare vnto my wofull cry.
Refuse me not that am vniust,
    but bowing downe thy heauenly eye.
Behold how I do still lament,
    my sinnes wherein I do offend,
O Lord for them shall I be shent:
    Sith thee to please I do intend.

No, no, not so, thy will is bent,
    to deale with sinners in thine ire:
But when in hart they shall repent,
    thou grauntst with speede their iust desire.
To thee therefore still shall I cry,
    to washe away my sinfull crime:
Thy bloud O Lord is not yet dry,
    but that it may helpe me in time.

Hast thee O Lord, hast thee I say,
    to poure on me the giftes of grace,
That when this life must flit away,
    in heauen with thee I may haue place.
Where thou doost raigne eternally,
    with God which once did downe thee send,
Where aungels sing continually,
    to thee be praise world without end.

Because of the narrow range at the beginning and the use of so much stepwise motion, the tune is more characteristic of plainsong than any of the other tunes for hymns in the Psalter. It is the clearly defined rhythmic pattern which removes it from the realm of Gregorian Chant, thus making it acceptable for the reformers. It is interesting to see how each phrase, except for the fourth, reaches a note a step higher than the preceding phrase, until the last when the curve drops down gently to the end. Again the Dorian mode is used.

The Residue of all Dauids Psalmes in metre, made by John Hopkins and others, with apt notes to syng them withal is dated 1562 and is bound with the Sternhold and Hopkins "first parte" in the Boston

Public Library volume. The title page of this rare Psalter does not bear the name of Thomas Sternhold and none of his work is found in it.[1] The seventy-six Psalms in this volume supply those which are lacking in the Sternhold and Hopkins "first parte" and duplicate, with different versification, Psalms 50, 51, 100, 117, 125, and 134. The only canticle is the *Song of the Three Children* which, in the Sternhold and Hopkins "first parte," is the sole omission from the canticles in general use. The only freely composed hymn is *The Humble Sute of the Sinner*. This is marked with a large letter M, probably signifying Markant as the author.

Example 6.

The Humble Sute of the Sinner
"O Lord of whō I do depend"
[First publication 1562]
C.M.D.
abcbdefe

John Hopkins, *The Residue of all Dauids Psalms*, 1562, pp. 194-196.

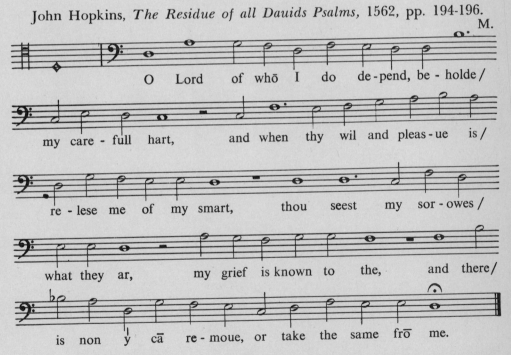

[The tenth note, printed B in this edition, should be G, as shown by examination of the tune in other Psalters. All of the other B's were probably sung B-flat.]

1 See Appendix for table of contents.

THE HUMBLE SUTE OF THE SINNER
M.

O Lord of whō I do depend,
  beholde my carefull hart,
& when thy wil & pleasue is
  relese me of my smart,
thou seest my sorowes what they ar,
  my grief is known to the,
& there is non ẏ cā remoue,
  or take the same frō me.

But only thou whose ayde I craue,
  whose mercy still is prest
To ease all those that come to thee,
  for succour and for rest.
And sith thou seest my restles eyes,
  my teares and greuous grone,
Attende vnto my sute (O Lorde)
  marke well my plaint and mone.

For sinne hath so inclosed me
  and compast me aboute:
That I am now remediles,
  if mercy helpe not out.
For mortall man, can not release,
  or mitigate this payne:
But euen thy Christ my Lorde and god,
  which for my sinnes was slayne.

Whose blody woundes are yet to see,
  though not with mortall eye:
Yet doth thy sainctes beholde tham all,
  and so I trust shall I.
Though sinne doth hinder me a whyle,
  when thou shalt see it good:
I shall enioye the sight of hym
  and see his woundes and blood.

And as thine angels and they sainctes,
    doo now beholde the same:
So trust I to posces that place,
    with them to prayse thy name,
But whiles I liue here in this vale,
    where sinners doo frequent:
Assiste me euer with thy grace
    my sinnes still to lament.

Lest that I treade in sinners trace,
    and geue them my consent:
To dwell with them in wickednes,
    whereto nature is bent.
Only thy grace must be my staye,
    lest that I fall downe flat,
And being downe, then of my selfe
    cannot recouer that.

Wherefore this is yet once agayne,
    my sute and my request:
To graunt me pardon for my sinne,
    that I in thee may rest.
Then shall my hart, my tong and voyce,
    be instruments of prayse:
And in thy Churche and house of sainctes,
    sing Psalmes to thee alwayes.

The gentle undulating curves of the tune are typical of modal music. The leaps at the beginning of the first, second, and last phrases serve as unifying factors, and the repeated note at the high point of the last phrase intensifies the climax. This earliest version of the tune has the most beautiful arrangement of phrases: two long ones of fourteen syllables, one of eight and one of six, then finishing with another of fourteen. Later arrangements impede the natural flow of the melody by using a long note at the beginning and end of each phrase of the last part.[1]

[1] The tune for Psalm XXXV, the first Psalm in the Hopkins book, begins as this tune does, but is completely different after the fourth phrase. The tune for Psalm XXXV may be seen in Frost, *op. cit.*, p. 100, although the tune in the Hopkins Psalter does not agree rhythmically with the version shown by Mr. Frost.

These six hymns, then, were the first to be written originally in English[1] and published for the use of the congregation in the English church service, and although the number is small compared with the profusion of metered Psalms in the sixteenth century, even so, they held tenaciously to their position in the Sternhold and Hopkins Psalters for about 200 years. As lyric verse the hymns make no claim to literary distinction but they do provide opportunity to sing of Christ's love: an opportunity not furnished by the Psalms.

Three of the tunes are of uncommon beauty when sung as printed before the necessity for bar lines was felt. The "Short introduction into the Science of Musike" at the beginning of the Psalter explains that the notes of music were called long, breve, semibreve, minim, and crotchet. In this volume the value of each could be easily remembered, the reader is told, because in the order listed each note was equal to half the length of the note preceding it. The dot was equal to half the value of the note which it followed. Application of these rules shows that none of the tunes can be barred consistently within a single time signature, but the long and short notes follow each other in a free-flowing rhythm and with sensitive feeling for the meaning of the text.

Along with the tunes of Tallis and Gibbons, which have found a place in modern hymnals, these tunes, too, deserve to be restored to use.

---

[1] An English version of *Veni Creator* was in the Ordinal of 1550; the only translation of the Office hymns which was used at that time. Archbishop Cranmer translated *Salve festa dies* but in a letter to Henry VIII expressed some doubt of its worth, and the translation has not been preserved. (See Oliver Strunk, *Source Readings in Music History*, p. 350.)

THE RESIDVE

of all Dauids Psalmes in

metre, made by Iohn Hopkins and
others, with apt notes to syng them
withal. Faythfully perused and
alowed according to thordre
appointed in the Quenes
maiesties Iniunctiōs.

Nowe fyrst Imprinted and sette
forth in this fourme for such as haue
bookes alredy, that thei that be disposed
maye ioyne these wyth them: and so
to haue the whole Psalmes.

IAMES. V.

If any be afflicted, let him pray, and if anye
be merye let him singe Psalmes.

COLLOSS. III.

℥ Let the worde of G O D dwell plenteously in
all wysdome, teaching and exhortyng one another in psalmes Hymnes & spirituall son
ges and syng vnto the Lorde in your
heartes.

Imprinted at London by John Daye
dwellyng ouer Aldersgate.
Cum gratia & priuilegio Regiē Maiestatis, per septennium.
1562

Title page *The Residue of all Dauids Psalmes* (1562)

Harmonizations
of the Tunes

Behold this Table.

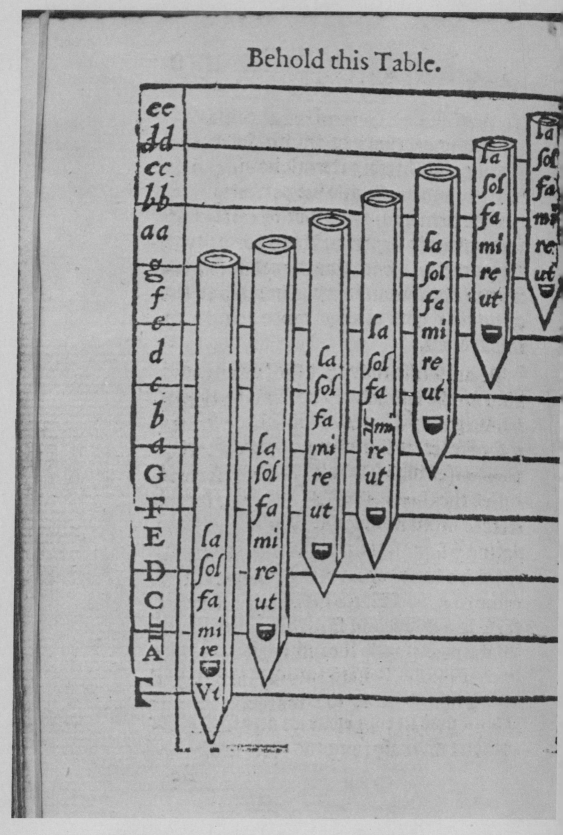

From "An Introduction to learne to sing" in *The first parte of the Booke of Psalmes*, Sternehold and Hopkins (1569)

CHAPTER III

LONG WITH THE Sternhold and Hopkins Psalters which present the hymn tunes as single melodic lines, various volumes of four-part settings of the tunes were published. The six hymns quoted in the preceding chapter were usually included in the books of harmonizations, and it is interesting to compare the modal harmonizations of the last half of the sixteenth century with the "modern" harmonic structures of the seventeenth century.

John Day was one of the first to publish the tunes in parts and his important volumes of 1563 give, before the Psalms, four versions of *The lamentation of a sinner*. One is by T. C., one by R. Brimle, and two by W. P.; the second of these being for men. There are two settings of *The humble sute*, T. C. and W. P. listed as composers, and T. Causton and R. Brimle each contribute one setting of *The complaint of a sinner*. After the Psalms, among various prayers, come three settings of *The complaint of a sinner*, all by W.P. Presumably, T.C. was Thomas Caustin, a gentleman of the Chapel Royal, represented in the *Wanley MS.* with some musical settings of the service in English, and in John Day's *Certaine notes set forthe in foure and three parts*, 1560.[1] Nothing

---

[1] Gustave Reese, *Music in the Renaissance*, New York, 1959, pp. 796-797.

seems to be known about Brimle. W. P. was William Parsons, assistant choirmaster and copyist at Wells Cathedral in 1551 where he remained for ten years. He was a contributor to the Ravenscroft Psalter of 1621.

The harmonizations in Day's *Whole psalms in foure partes*, 1563, were published in separate partbooks and only the tenor book was available to this writer. The tenor part carries the tune which, in the case of the hymn tunes, shows only a few changes from earlier editions. Each hymn is complete on one page and only one stanza is given with the music. Either the texts were well enough known to eliminate the need for printing all the stanzas, or the singers had to have another book available with the remaining stanzas.

In 1565 John Day published *Mornyng and Euenyng prayer and Communion, set forthe in foure partes to be song in churches, both for men and children wyth dyuers other godly prayers and Anthems, of sundry mens doynges*. This, too, was in separate part books. The bass part book carries the same title as the other parts, telling that the music is for both men and children but adds that it is also to play on instruments. In the collection, among various settings of canticles, prayers, and anthems is a harmonization by M. Talis of "O Lord in thee is all my trust."[1] All of the parts are marked "for children" although the range of them is the same as for four mixed voices.

Example 7.

A LAMENTATION
"O Lord in thee is all my trust"
M. Talis, *Mornyng and Euenyng prayer and Communion*, 1565.

[1] Same hymn found in *Certaine notes set forth in foure and three parts . . . 1560.*

[The blackened note at the end of the second system in the contratenor should
be sung as a half-note. The whole-notes with the words *thē* in meane, tenor and
bassus in the fifth system, and *shent* in the last system should be sung as dotted
whole-notes because they are perfected by the following three half-notes. The
whole-note, nine notes from the end in the contratenor, is misprinted in the
Psalter and should be a half-note.]

The next edition of harmonizations published by John Day was the work of one composer, William Damon. This came out in 1579, and the now well-known explanation of the way in which these settings reached the publisher is given in the Preface of a 1591 publication of Damon. In the later book published after Damon's death through the efforts of his friend William Swayne, the reader is told

> Heretofore gentle Reader, M. William Damon one of her Maiesties Musitions, being earnestly requested by a friend of his did at sundry times when he resorted to his friends house compose the tunes of Dauids Psalms as they are ordinarily soung in the Church note for note, intending thē for his friends priuate use. These Psalmes so set and made without labour or purpose to publish them, were notwithstanding published by the same friend of M. Damon; which not answering thexpectation that many had of the Auctors skill, gaue him occasion to take uppon him a new labour to recouer the wrong his friend did in publishing that that was so done, as might well please him, but was not purposed or framed for the learned eares of our times. Therefore at his best leisure . . . he composed the same tunes again. . . . Now . . . he hath for varietie gone through the Psalmes twice, which are now deuided into two Setts: where of in the former the ordinaire singing part is carried in the Tenor: In the second set it is convueyed in the highest part.[1]

This, then, is the explanation of the rather apologetic foreward by Edward Hake in the first Damon book, 1579, where the public is told that John Bull procured the music "piece meale" from William Damon, who did not know it was to be published. The music in the unauthorized Damon collection is, as the composer suspected, only tolerable. For this reason only two harmonizations of hymn tunes will be shown even though all six of the hymns and tunes under discussion are in the volume. In all of the harmonizations there is little real melodic interest in the parts accompanying the tenor, where the tune is generally placed. The low range of the added parts is to be noted, particularly in "O Lord turn not thy face away" where the contratenor is beneath the tenor a great deal of the time. The rhythm has not yet been forced into a strait jacket.

---

[1] William Damon, *The second Booke of Musicke,* Cantus [Part], 1591, Preface.

34

Example 8.

The humble sute of a Sinner
"O Lord of whō I do depend"
Guilielmo Daman, *The Psalmes of David in English meter, with
Notes of foure partes set vnto them,* 1579, pp. 2-3.
S.T.C. 6219

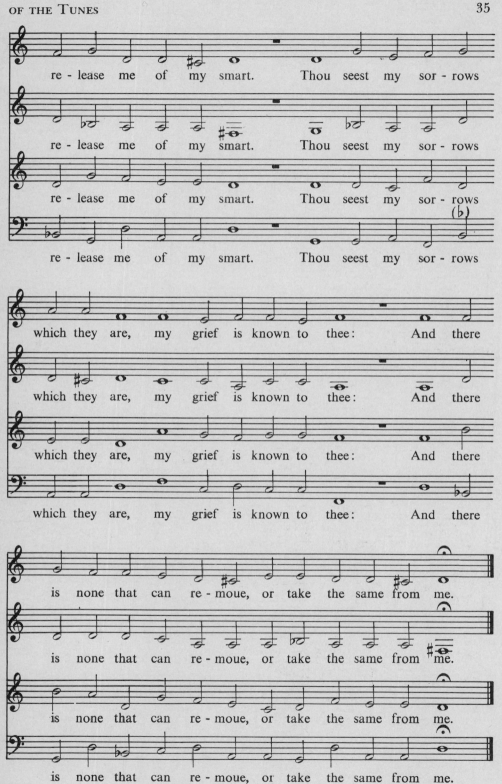

re - lease me   of   my   smart.   Thou seest my   sor - rows

re - lease me   of   my   smart.   Thou seest my   sor - rows

re - lease me   of   my   smart.   Thou seest my   sor - rows

re - lease me   of   my   smart.   Thou seest my   sor - rows

which they are,   my   grief is known to   thee: And   there

which they are,   my   grief is known to   thee: And   there

which they are,   my   grief is known to   thee: And   there

which they are,   my   grief is known to   thee: And   there

is   none that can   re - moue,   or take   the same from   me.

is   none that can   re - moue,   or take   the same from   me.

is   none that can   re - moue,   or take   the same from   me.

is   none that can   re - moue,   or take   the same from   me.

Morley's treatise on theory prohibits the use of both the fifth and sixth above the bass, as in the fifth chord from the end, except when treated as a two/three suspension in the cadence.[1]

Example 9.

The Lamentation of a Sinner
"O Lorde turne not thy face away"
Guilielmo Daman, *The Psalmes of David in English meter, with Notes of foure partes set vnto them,* 1579, p. 10.
S.T.C. 6219

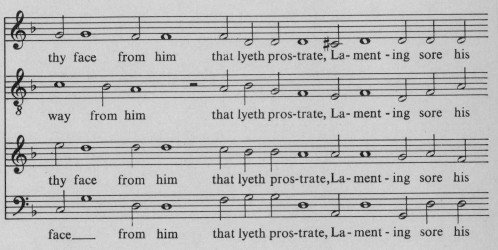

---

[1] Thomas Morley, *A Plain and Easy Introduction to Practical Music,* New York, [1953], p. 243.

Similar motion to the fifth between the bass and the highest part with the latter part leaping at the words "before" and "that do" are perhaps reasons for Mr. Damon's embarrassment in having the settings published.

While it may be unfair to Damon not to show some work from his two sets of harmonizations published in 1591, in which he hoped to repair the damage done to his reputation as a composer by the publishing of the earlier volume, nevertheless, none will be given. The 1591 settings are in motet style and could not have been useful for congregational singing. There is no indication that the first volume was so used either, but if one had chosen to use it for this purpose the simplicity of the music would have made it practical.

The next important publication of harmonizations of the church tunes was in 1592. A copy of the third edition of this book, printed by Thomas Este for the Company of Stationers in 1604, was used as the source for the following versions of the hymn tunes. The title, in part, was *The Whole Booke of Psalmes With Their Wonted Tunes, as they are sung in Churches, composed into foure parts: . . . . Compiled by X Svndry Avthors, who haue so laboured heerin, that the vnskilful with small practice may attaine to sing that part, which is fittest for their voyce.*

The title page is decorated in ornate style and figures representing the two apostles Matthew and Mark dominate the columns which mark the side margins; Matthew at the left and Mark at the right.

The music is printed on a double page. The cantus, with words of the first stanza of the hymn beneath the notes, and tenor, with words of the first stanza repeated, are on the left page; the altus and bassus in corresponding position on the right page. Remaining stanzas are printed without music. When tune or hymn is not complete on one page, all parts turn together.

An index of eight "new" tunes shows the first notes of each along with the composer's name. The added information is given that the first four of the tunes were used in most churches of the realm. These "popular" ones are by J. Dowland, E. Blancks, E. Hooper, and R. Hooper. The remaining ones are by J. Farmer, who harmonized all of the hymns and canticles before the Psalms, and R. Allison, G. Kirby, and J. Fanner. The tune which is attributed here to E. Hooper and given with *A*

Prayer unto the holy ghost actually had been used in the Damon book of 1579.[1]

This was the golden age of the English secular song, and it was to the most skillful composers of madrigals, balletts, and ayres that Este turned for harmonizations of the church tunes. The results of their labors show that no different skill from that used in writing secular songs is needed to write successfully for the church service. The tunes used for the hymns are all harmonized in a plain fashion but with independence and melodic interest in all voice parts.

Example 10.

The Lamentation of a Sinner
Harmonization by J. Farmer
Thomas Este, *The Whole Booke of Psalmes*, 3rd ed., 1604, pp. 18-19.
S.T.C. 2515

Cantvs

O Lorde turne not a - way thy face,

Altvs

O Lorde turne not a - way thy face,

Tenor

O Lorde turne not a - way thy face,

Bassvs

O Lorde turne not a - way thy face,

---

[1] Frost, *op. cit.*, p. 86.

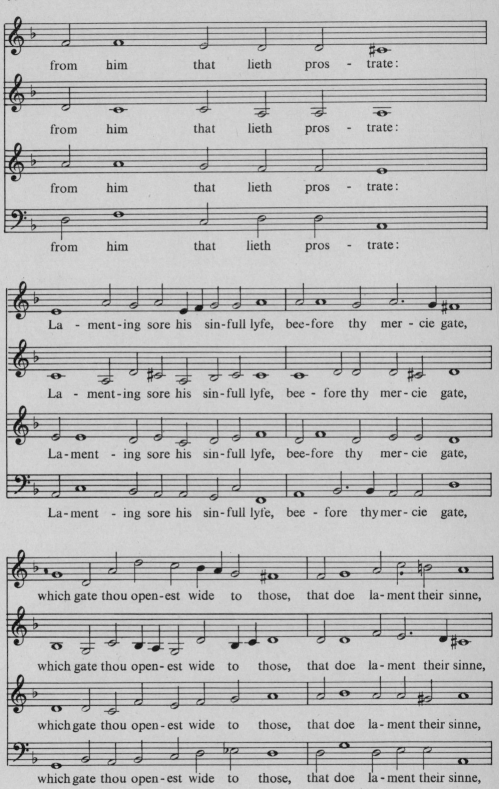

from him that lieth pros - trate:

from him that lieth pros - trate:

from him that lieth pros - trate:

from him that lieth pros - trate:

La - ment-ing sore his sin-full lyfe, bee-fore thy mer - cie gate,

La - ment-ing sore his sin-full lyfe, bee - fore thy mer - cie gate,

La - ment - ing sore his sin-full lyfe, bee-fore thy mer - cie gate,

La - ment - ing sore his sin-full lyfe, bee - fore thy mer - cie gate,

which gate thou open-est wide to those, that doe la-ment their sinne,

which gate thou open-est wide to those, that doe la-ment their sinne,

which gate thou open-est wide to those, that doe la-ment their sinne,

which gate thou open-est wide to those, that doe la-ment their sinne,

shut not   that gate a-gainst me Lord,   but let mee   en - ter in.

shut not   that gate a-gainst me Lord, but   let   mee en - ter in.

shut not   that gate a-gainst me Lord,   but   let   mee en-ter   in.

shut not that   gate a - gainst me Lord,   but   let   mee en-ter   in.

[The F-sharp in the first system of the cantus, printed a half-note in the Psalter, should be a whole-note. The D in the tenor, third system, ninth note, is an obvious misprint for E.]

John Farmer (fl. 1591-1601) wrote a little treatise on three-part counterpoint in addition to his composition of madrigals. The interest in his harmonization of *The Lamentation of a Sinner* lies in the variety of chords used, a characteristic of modal writing. In the third bar there is a cross-relation, where for a moment the music seems to modulate to F major. The use of the cross-relation is common in English music of this period although not acceptable in the "pure" Palestrina style of the same period. All of the cadences end with a major third except the last where no third is found, and in all but one of the cadences using the third, it is placed in the cantus. The cantus part competes quite successfully for melodic interest with the tenor which carries the tune. Each part has an octave range within which the cantus reaches its highest note twice; the tenor only once. The largest leaps, a minor sixth, perfect fifth, and two perfect fourths, are found at the beginning of phrases in the cantus.

Example 11.

A praier to the holy Ghost
Harmonization by E. Hooper
Thomas Este, *The Whole Booke of Psalmes*, 3rd ed., 1604, pp. 226-267.
Tune from Daman 1579, used with Psalm XXIII.[1]
S.T.C. 2515

1 Frost, *op. cit.*, p. 86.

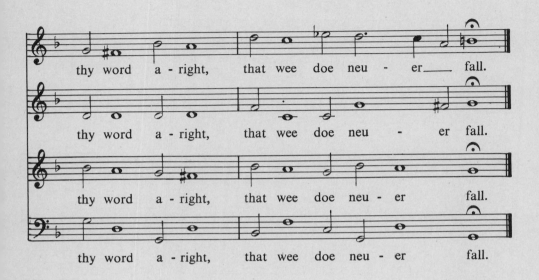

thy word   a - right,   that wee   doe   neu - er___   fall.

thy word   a - right,   that wee   doe   neu -   er   fall.

thy word   a - right,   that wee   doe   neu - er   fall.

thy word   a - right,   that wee   doe   neu - er   fall.

Edmund Hooper (c. 1553-1621) was organist at Westminster
Abbey in 1606. He is represented in the *Fitzwilliam Virginal Book* by
an Alman, No. CCXXVII, and a Corranto, No. CCXXVIII. He also
composed anthems and services.

The tune here has been taken from the early Damon collection and
the double common meter of the first tune for the hymn abandoned,
the music now accommodating the hymn in four-line stanzas. There is
an interesting use of a diminished fourth in the tenor at the words
"aright that." The interval, forbidden at the time, is the result of
making the third above the bass major in the cadence at the end of the
fourth bar. Its effect is heightened as it is made the central part of a
five-note imitative passage between cantus and tenor, begun in the
cantus. There are octaves between the altus and bassus just before the
final cadence.

Example 12.

The Complainte of a sinner
Harmonization by J. Farmer
Thomas Este, *The Whole Booke of Psalmes,* 3rd ed., 1604, pp. 22-25.
S.T.C. 2515

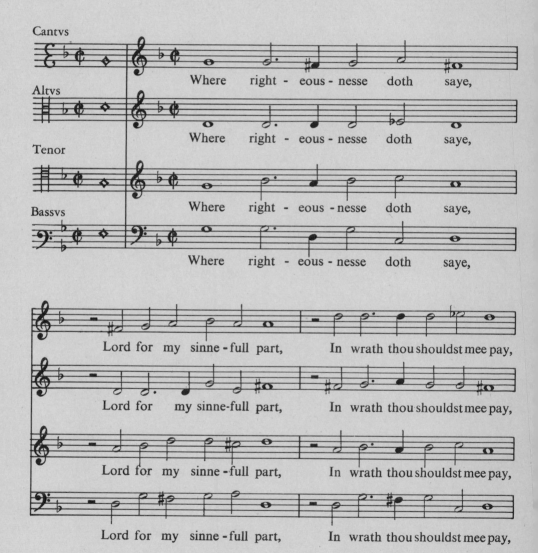

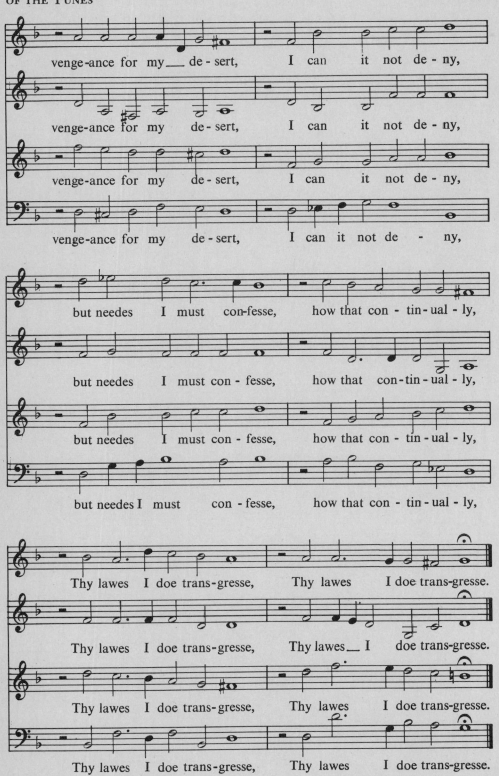

For the most part this music is closer to G minor and B-flat major than to the first mode transposed. It is towards the end that the modal flavor is retained. The last phrase of this tune was difficult for most composers to handle, and Allison's solution, Example 17, is the most successful. Farmer uses two examples of the voice leading which was frowned on by Morley in his *Plain and Easy Introduction to Practical Music,* and he warned his student against "some such quiditie"[1] as composers of madrigals often wrote in that form of music and which he thought had no place in motets. One of these is in bar four where there are ill-concealed octaves between cantus and altus. The other is the approach by leap to the fifth between outer parts in bar five. Notice also, the ubiquitous cross-relation within the phrase in bar four.

Example 13.

A Thankesgiuing
Harmonization by I. Douland
Thomas Este, *The Whole Booke of Psalmes,* 3rd ed., 1604, pp. 270-273.
Tune from Scottish 1564/65, used with Psalm CVIII.[2]
S.T.C. 2515

---

[1] Morley, *op. cit.,* p. 253.
[2] Frost, *op. cit.,* p. 154.

I. Douland is, of course, the renowned John Dowland (1563-1626), composer of secular songs and lute music, and from 1598-1607 lutanist to the King of Denmark. The tune for *A Thankesgiuing*, credited to Dowland in the Este volume, was taken from the Scottish Psalter 1564/65.[1] Its range is very limited and the third phrase is like the first phrase

[1] Frost, *op. cit.*, p. 154.

reversed. All of the parts which Dowland·has written hold more interest than the Psalm tune. The cantus, especially, with its flowing curve out-shines the tenor. The repetition of the three notes in all parts at the end of the first and third phrases is unusual for this period, as is the final cadence which does not use a suspension but strikes all notes of the "dominant" chord together. A bold dissonance is seen in the altus part, fifth note, for suspensions and passing tones were the rule at this time.

Example 14.

The Lamentation
Harmonization by George Kirby
Thomas Este, *The Whole Booke of Psalmes,* 3rd ed., 1604, pp. 268-271.
S.T.C. 2515

George Kirby's first known work is his contribution to the Este book which includes harmonizations for *The Lords praier,* the *Creed,* and some Psalm tunes as well as the *Lamentation.* Before his death in 1634 he distinguished himself as one of the best madrigal writers of his time and his works in this form are republished in Vol. **XXIV** of the *English Madrigal School.*

There is more variety in the dissonance used here than in the other harmonizations of hymn tunes in Este. Both four/three and seven/six suspensions are used, and more passing tones are found. Both upper and lower auxiliaries appear. The much used four-note figure of the sixteenth-century cambiata is shown in the altus, bar two; and in the cantus of the same bar, an example of a "neighboring tone."

Kirby, like the other madrigal writers who harmonized church tunes for Este, shows little concern for the kind of motion used in the approach to a fifth between outer voices (note the penultimate bar), or for the use of successive octaves in contrary motion (note the last bar).

Example 15.

The humble sute of a sinner
Harmonization by I. Farmer
Thomas Este, *The Whole Booke of Psalmes,* 3rd ed., 1604, pp. 4-5.
S.T.C. 2515

be - hold   my   care - full   hart:

be - hold   my   care - full   hart:

be - hold   my   care - full   hart:

be - hold   my   care - full   hart:

&   when thy will & ple - sure is,   re - lease   me of my smart,

&   when thy will & ple - sure is,   re - lease me of   my smart,

&   when   thy will & ple - sure is,   re - lease   me of my smart,

&   when thy will & ple - sure is,   re - lease   me of my smart,

Thou   seest my sor-rowes what they are,   my   griefe is knowne to thee,

Thou   seest my sor-rowes what they are,   my griefe is   knowne   to thee,

Thou   seest my sor-rowes what they are,   my   griefe is knowne to thee,

Thou seest   my sor-rowes what they are,   my   griefe is knowne to thee,

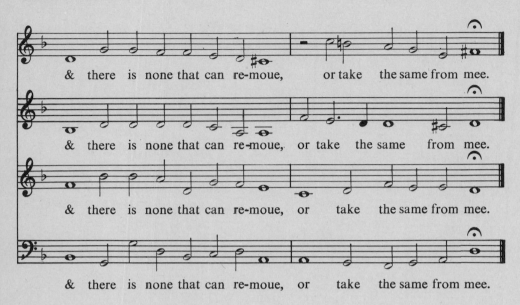

& there is none that can re-moue, or take the same from mee.

& there is none that can re-moue, or take the same from mee.

& there is none that can re-moue, or take the same from mee.

& there is none that can re-moue, or take the same from mee.

The fourth chord in the fourth bar sounds like the first inversion of a seventh chord on ii with the seventh introduced as a suspension, and then the supertonic seventh resolves with "tonal" voice leading to the dominant. Surrounded by successions of chords in modal style, this brief effect of tonality is quite beautiful. The cadence is repeated at the end of the tune. The leap of a diminished octave in the highest part just before the last bar is more demanding of the singer than these tunes usually are, even though the skip comes between phrases separated by a rest.

Another important Psalter with harmonizations followed soon after the Este of 1592. This came out in 1599, and all the music was by Richard Allison. Unfortunately, Dr. Burney did not appreciate the smooth-flowing beauty of the part writing and said scornfully of it

> If the author's friends may be credited, who have written verses in praise of the work, it abounds with uncommon excellence. However, the puff-direct, in the shape of friendly panegyrics prefixed to books, was no more to be depended on by the public in Queen Elizabeth's time, than the puffs oblique of present newspapers. The book has no merit, but what was common, at the time it was printed.[1]

Wooldridge observes in his article on the Psalter in *Grove's Dictionary*

[1] Charles A. Burney, *A General History of Music,* London, 1789, Vol. III, p. 57.

that the purity of style of Allison's writing should not be considered less praiseworthy simply because such music was common at that time. Harmonizations of the four hymn tunes in the volume are reproduced here in order that the music may be seen outside of the rare book room, even though the music is not quite as interesting as that found in the Este Psalter.

The title of the book reveals the instruments which might have been used with a single singing voice. *The Psalmes of Dauid in Meter, The plaine Song beeing the common tunne to be sung and plaide vpon the Lute, Orpharyon, Citterne, or Base Violl, seuerally or altogether. The singing part to be either Tenor or Treble to the Instrument, according to the nature of the voyce, or for fowre voyces . . . By Richard Allison . . . 1599.*

The book is a folio edition arranged so that the musicians can be seated around a table. The cantus reads from the bottom of the left page. The part is the church tune, and the singer can, if he chooses, accompany himself on the lute, as the tablature for that instrument is printed below his part. The tune may be sung by a treble at the pitch written or by a tenor an octave lower when accompanied by instruments. On the opposite side of the table is the citterne player reading his part from the top of the left page without turning the book.

If no instruments are used four voice parts are available. The cantus reads from the bottom of the left page but sings only at the pitch written, as a tenor part is supplied at the bottom of the right page. The center of the right page gives the part for the bassus facing the side of the table at the tenor's right. The altus part is at the top of the right page, placing this singer opposite the tenor.

Example 16.

The Lamentation
Harmonization by Richard Allison
Richard Allison, *The Psalmes of Dauid in Meter,* 1599, unpaged.
S.T.C. 2407

which gate thou open-est wide to those, that do   la - ment their sinne,

which gate thou open-est wide to those, that do   la - ment their sinne,

which gate   thou open-est wide to those, that do   la - ment their sinne,

which gate   thou open-est wide to those, that do   la - ment their sinne,

shut not   that gate   a - gainst me Lord, but let   me en - ter in.

shut not   that gate___   a-gainst me Lord, but let me   en - ter in.

shut not that   gate   a - gainst me Lord, but let   me___ en - ter   in.

shut not that gate   a - gainst me Lord, but let   me __ en - ter   in.

Notice the fine ascending lines in the tenor and bassus leading into the final cadence, and how the final cadence makes use of the expected four/three suspension but the octave above the bass in the penultimate chord does not descend through a seventh to the third above the last note of the bass. Thus the composition ends with the archaic sound of a chord without a third.

Example 17.

The complaint of a Sinner
Harmonization by Richard Allison
Richard Allison, *The Psalmes of Dauid in Meter,* 1599, unpaged.
S.T.C. 2407

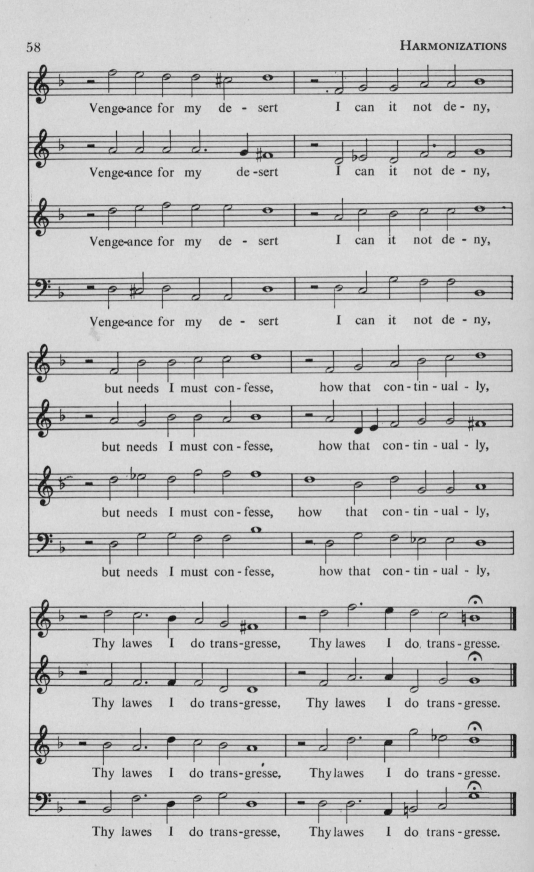

Venge-ance for my de - sert   I can it not de - ny,

Venge-ance for my   de -sert   I can it not de - ny,

Venge-ance for my de - sert   I can it not de - ny,

Venge-ance for my de - sert   I can it not de - ny,

but needs I must con - fesse,   how that con - tin - ual - ly,

but needs I must con - fesse,   how that con - tin - ual - ly,

but needs I must con - fesse,   how that con - tin - ual - ly,

but needs I must con - fesse,   how that con - tin - ual - ly,

Thy lawes I do trans-gresse,   Thy lawes I do. trans - gresse.

Thy lawes I do trans-gresse,   Thy lawes I do trans - gresse.

Thy lawes I do trans-gresse,   Thy lawes I do trans - gresse.

Thy lawes I do trans-gresse,   Thy lawes I do trans - gresse.

The dotted note pattern found here and in the Farmer harmonization from Este's Psalter is a change in rhythm from the first two phrases of the original tune. In bars five and six there is the impression of a melodic sequence although actually there is none. The altus moves above the cantus for one note at the beginning of bar six to give the sequential effect. The final cadence is successfully handled by Allison's substitution of the subdominant chord for the leading-tone chord used in the Farmer harmonization, and by the anticipation of the major third of the last chord with B-natural, third bass note from the end.

Example 18.

A Lamentation
Richard Allison, *The Psalmes of Dauid in Meter*, 1599, unpaged.
S.T.C. 2407

fuse me not that am un-iust, but bow-ing down thy heaven-ly eye, Be-

fuse me not that am un - iust, but bow-ing down thy heaven-ly eye, Be-

fuse me not that am un - iust, but bow-ing down thy heaven-ly eye, Be-

fuse me not that am un - iust, but bow-ing down thy heaven-ly eye, Be-

hold how I do still la - ment, my sinnes where-in I doe of-fend : O

hold how I do still la-ment, my sinnes where-in I doe of - fend : O

hold how I do still la - ment, my sinnes where-in I doe of - fend : O

hold how I do still la - ment, my sinnes where - in I doe— of- fend : O

Lord for them shall I be shent, Sith thee to please I do in - tend.

Lord for them shall I be shent, Sith thee to please I do in-tend.

Lord for them shall I be shent, Sith thee to please I do in - tend.

Lord for them shall I be shent, Sith thee to please— I do in - tend.

Example 19.

The humble sute of a sinner
Harmonization by Richard Allison
Richard Allison, *The Psalmes of Dauid in Meter,* 1599, unpaged.
S.T.C. 2407

and when thy will and pleas-ure is, re-lease me of my smart.

and when thy will and pleas-ure is, re-lease me of my smart.

and when thy will and pleas-ure is, re-lease me of my smart.

and when thy will and pleas-ure is, re-lease me of my smart.

Thou seest my sor-rowes what they are, my griefe is knowne to thee,

Thou seest my sor-rowes what they are, my griefe is knowne to thee,

Thou seest my sor-rowes what they are, my griefe is knowne to thee,

Thou seest my sor-rowes what they are, my griefe is knowne to thee,

And there is none that can re-move, or take the same from me.

And there is none that can re-move, or take the same from me.

And there is none that can re-move, or take the same from me.

And there is none that can re-move, or take the same from me.

The seventh bar is not an example of Allison's best writing with thinly disguised octaves between tenor and cantus at the beginning of the bar, an unprepared seventh in the fifth note of the altus, and moving on from the same spot, fifths between cantus and tenor. In the last bar, above the second bass note, there is a fifth and sixth together with the momentary sound of a diminished seventh chord in first inversion. In spite of these minor infractions of the rules of sixteenth-century contrapuntal writing, Allison is generally a fine craftsman, and these examples of his writing show independence and beauty of individual lines.

The peak of the pure Elizabethan style of simple harmonizations had been reached with Este's Psalter and Allison attempted to maintain it. The hymns continued in use but following books of harmonizations of the tunes show a deterioration in style and refinement as the later chordal style became established. The preponderance of tonic and dominant chords added to the uniformity of rhythmic patterns neatly enclosed in bar lines produced a kind of setting best illustrated by examples from Ravenscroft and Playford, the outstanding Psalters of the seventeenth and eighteenth centuries.

Example 20.

The Lamentation
Harmonization by Will. Parsons
Thomas Rauenscroft, *The Whole Booke of Psalmes*, 1621, pp. 18-19.
S.T.C. 2575

Shut not that gate a-gainst me Lord, but let me en - ter in.

Shut not that gate a-gainst me Lord, but let me en - ter in.

Shut not that gate a-gainst me Lord, but let me en - ter in.

Shut not that gate a-gainst me Lord, but let me en - ter in.

This is an altered version of the harmonization which Parsons did for Day's *Whole Psalter,* 1563. The next to last bar shows a clear F major harmonization of a phrase that retained modal flavor in both Este and Allison. The final cadence was probably sung with a B-natural in the medius, but where the same figure is used in bar four, the cross-relation the B-natural produces with the B-flat in the cantus is particularly harsh. The voice leading in the cadence shows the loss of purity in style which began at this time. As a melody, the cantus leaves much to be desired as it goes to its highest note four times, and the constant use of repeated notes hinders the forward movement.

Example 21.

A Prayer to the holy Ghost
Harmonization by John Milton
Thomas Rauenscroft, *The Whole Booke of Psalmes*, 1621, pp. 266-267.
Yorke Tune [from *Scottish Psalter*, 1615, called The Stilt.[1]]

1 Frost, *op. cit.*, p. 256.

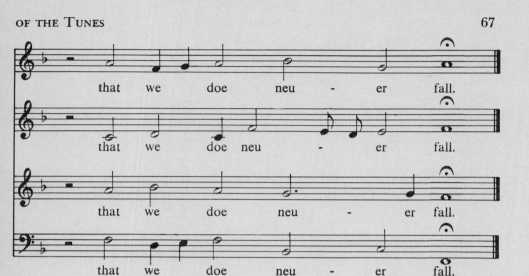

John Milton (c. 1563-1646/47) was the father of the poet. His musical compositions were all choral pieces and his writing, as shown in this harmonization, was based on sound musicianship even if somewhat lacking in inspiration. The tune for *A Prayer to the holy Ghost* was named Yorke in the Ravenscroft volume. It is a single common meter tune, a more popular meter in the seventeenth century than the double common meter, and uses the type of final cadence which is characteristic of the Psalter. F major is clearly defined.

Example 22.

The Complaint of a sinner
Harmonization by Rauenscroft
Thomas Rauenscroft, *The Whole Booke of Psalmes*, 1621, pp. 22-25.
S.T.C. 2575

In wrath thou shouldst me pay   venge-ance for my de - sert.

In wrath thou shouldst me pay   venge-ance for my de - sert.

In   wrath thou shouldst me pay   venge-ance for my de - sert.

In wrath thou shouldst me pay   venge-ance for my de - sert.

I can it not de - ny,   but needs   I must   con-fesse,

I can it not de - ny,   but needs I must___ con - fesse,

I can it not de - ny,   but needs I must   con - fesse,

I can it not de - ny,   but needs I must   con - fesse,

how that   con -tin - ual - ly   Thy lawes I doe   trans-gresse.

how that con - tin - ual - ly   Thy lawes   I doe trans-gresse.

how that   con -tin - ual - ly   Thy lawes   I doe trans gresse.

how that   con -tin - ual - ly   Thy lawes   I doe trans-gresse.

Thomas Ravenscroft (c. 1590—c. 1633) was awarded the Bachelor of Music degree at Cambridge in 1607. His musical activities included a four-year term as music-master at Christ's Hospital and editorial work of some importance. *Pammelia,* which came out in 1609, was a collection of rounds, catches, and fragments of popular tunes. In the same year he published *Deuteromelia,* a collection of rounds and *Freeman's Songs,* which included *Three Blind Mice.* His name is probably best known, however, for the Psalter from which this hymn and Examples 20, 21, 23, and 24 are quoted.

The music reproduced here is typical of Ravenscroft's writing in the Psalter. His harmonization of *A Lamentation* is given in Example 24.

Example 23.

A Thankesgiuing
Harmonization by Simon Stubbs
Thomas Rauenscroft, *The Whole Booke of Psalmes,* 1621, pp. 270-273.
Martyrs Tune first used in *Scottish,* 1615.[1]
S.T.C. 2575

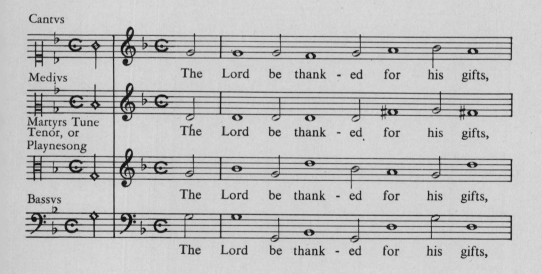

Cantvs

The Lord be thank - ed for his gifts,

Medivs

The Lord be thank - ed for his gifts,

Martyrs Tune
Tenor, or
Playnesong

The Lord be thank - ed for his gifts,

Bassvs

The Lord be thank - ed for his gifts,

[1] Frost, *op. cit.,* p. 257.

[The two blackened notes in the last bar of the cantus should probably be sung as two whole-notes.]

Example 24.

The Lamentation
Harmonization by Tho. Rauenscroft
Thomas Rauenscroft, *The Whole Booke of Psalmes,* 1621, pp. 268-271.
S.T.C. 2575

Cantvs

O Lord   in   thee is   all my___ trust,   giue

Medivs

Tenor, or
Playnesong

O   Lord in   thee   is   all   my trust, giue

O   Lord   in . thee   is   all   my trust, giue

Bassvs

O   Lord   in . thee   is   all   my trust, giue

eare vn-to my wo-full cry: Re-fuse me not that am un - iust,

eare vn-to my wo-full cry: Re-fuse me not that am un-iust,

eare vn-to my wo-full cry: Re-fuse me not that am un - iust,

eare vn-to my wo-full cry: Re-fuse me not that am un - iust,

but bow-ing   downe thy heauen-ly eye.   Be-hold how I doe still la-ment

but bow - ing downe thy heauen-ly eye.   Be-hold how I doe still la-ment

but bow - ing downe thy heauen - ly eye.   Be-hold how I doe still la-ment

but bow - ing downe thy heauen-ly eye.   Be-hold how I doe still la-ment

Example 25.

The humble sute of the sinner
Harmonization by Robert Palmer
Thomas Rauenscroft, *The Whole Booke of Psalmes,* 1621, pp. 4-5.
S.T.C. 2575

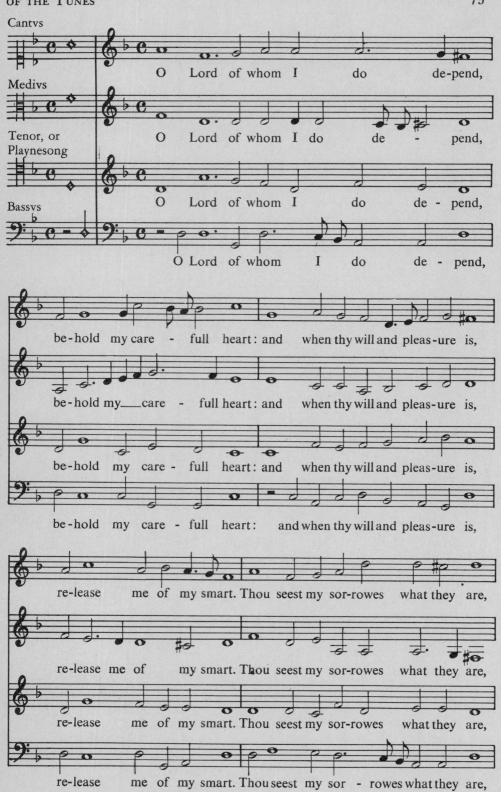

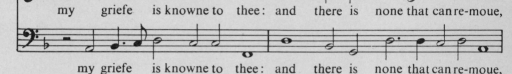

my   griefe   is knowne to thee: and   there is   none that can re-moue,

my griefe is knowne   to   thee: and there   is none that can re-moue,

my   griefe   is knowne to   thee: and   there is   none that can re-moue,

my griefe   is knowne to   thee: and   there is   none that can re-moue,

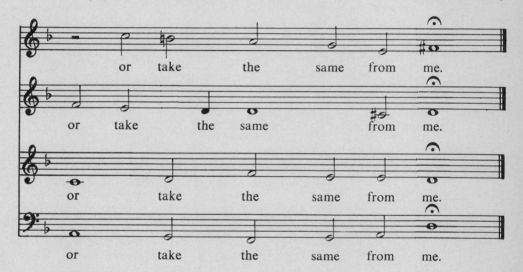

or   take   the   same   from   me.

or   take   the   same   from   me.

or   take   the   same   from   me.

or   take   the   same   from   me.

The resemblance between this harmonization of the *Humble Sute* and that by Farmer in the Este Psalter[1] is apparent. Some measures are identical. In other spots the altus of the Farmer becomes the cantus of the Palmer. The differences are principally in word settings. The parts no longer coincide so that all will sing the same word at the same time. This is seen particularly in the bar with the words "my grief is known to thee." The medius in the Palmer setting sings a syllable to an eighth, which is a more advanced writing than the setting from which it is copied. In the first bar the two eighths were probably sung C-sharp and B-natural, and if the first syllable of "depend" is started on the eighth

[1] See Example 15.

C and used for three notes, the setting would conform to the rhythmic practice of the sixteenth century.

The Civil War broke out in 1642 and amid the political and religious turmoil which resulted there were no new publications of hymns. When Charles II was restored to the throne, however, the way was cleared for a renewal of congregational singing of better quality than the unaccompanied Psalm singing during the reign of Cromwell. The Earl of Selborne, in his book *Hymns Their History and Development,* cites two changes made when the Prayer Book was revised after the Restoration:

> In England two changes bearing on church hymnody were made, upon the revision of the Prayer-book after the Restoration, in 1661-1662. One was the addition of a shorter form of the Veni Creator. The other, and more important, was the insertion of the rubric after the third Collect at Morning and Evening Prayer: 'In quires and places where they sing, here followeth the Anthem.' By this rubric, synodical and parliamentary authority was given for the interruption, . . . of the prescribed order . . . by singing an anthem. . . . Those actually used . . . were, from the first, hymns in verse, as well as unmetrical passages of Scripture. . . . The word 'anthem' had no technical significance which could be an obstacle to the use under this rubric of metrical hymns.[1]

The kind of hymn that was used is found in John Playford's *Psalms and Hymns,* 1671. Playford (1623—c. 1686) was a music publisher of considerable importance during the mid-seventeenth century. Moreover, he was actively and sincerely interested in restoring congregational singing to the level it had reached before the time of the Commonwealth. He served as clerk to the Temple Church and in the Preface of the 1671 edition of *Psalms and Hymns* laments the fact that many other clerks were trying to perform their duties with inadequate musical qualifications. The volume contains forty-seven tunes, long and short. The Common tunes are all in the tenor and may be sung to an organ, lute, or viol. Furthermore, Playford says

> To have this Musick more full and solemn, I have Compos'd to them two other parts, viz. Two Contratenors. All Four Parts moving to-

[1] Roundell Palmer, Earl of Selbourne, *Hymns Their History and Development,* London, 1892, pp. 151-152.

gether, being Composed to mens Voyces, and each Part in such a
Compass of Notes as may be performed with ordinary Voyces: And
in such places where there is Treble Voyces, those may sing the Tenor
or Common Tunes.[1]

There are two hymns, canticles, and two versions of *Veni Creator*
before the Psalms. Fifteen hymns are interspersed among the Psalms,
and three of the six solo songs at the end are hymns. Playford believed
that for the most part the authors of the hymns were unknown, but at
least fourteen are by John Austin and taken from his *Devotions in the
Antient Way of Offices,* 1668, and one is a translation of a Latin hymn.
George Herbert and Francis Quarles are also represented. Playford includes none of the first six English hymns.

In 1677 Playford issued a second Psalter. This was *The Whole
Book of Psalms: with The usual Hymns and Spiritual Songs; together
with all the ancient and proper Tunes sung in Churches, with some of
later use. Compos'd in Three Parts, Cantus, Medius, and Bassus: In a
more Plain and Useful Method than hath been formerly published. By
John Playford. . . . London Printed by W. Godbid for the Company of
Stationers . . . 1677.*
The Preface, as in the earlier book, is given over to the defense of
singing Psalms and hymns in the church service, and the reasons for the
deterioration in congregational singing. One of the reasons was the ill
custom of reading every line by itself before it was sung; a custom, the
author says, which originated in Scotland. The procedure resulted in
stops and stays which were highly objectionable. Disasters occurred when
the clerk, responsible for giving each line to the congregation before it
was sung, missed a line. The result might be not enough notes in the
next line of music to accommodate the words. The chaos was especially
bad when an organ was used for accompaniment, as was frequently
done. Before clerk, organist, and congregation could be brought together again with correct notes and words, the hymn had lost its meaning and religious value. The author concludes that the whole custom
was unnecessary in London because there "you have not three in a
hundred but can read." Playford also commends the parish clerks in
London who had recently set up an organ in their Common-Hall, and

---

[1] John Playford, *Psalms & Hymns in Solemn Musick of Foure Parts,* London, 1671, Preface.
unpaged.

met once a fortnight with an organist to play for them, in order to practice the singing of Psalms and hymns.

The book prints the tunes arranged

> into Three parts, viz. Cantus, Medius, and Bassus. All knowing persons in the Science will confess, that All Parts of Musick are contained in Three. . . . This [arrangement] more useful than Four, and easier perform'd.[1]

The composer says that the medius was written so that it would not rise above the Church tune in the treble, "or cloud it except in such places as it could not be well avoided." As will be seen in the music, such places are rather numerous! The bass was made suitable for "indifferent voice" and all three parts could be sung by men, or boys, or women. Accompaniment could be played on organ, lute, or viol.

There are only six freely composed hymns in this book, a curtailment from the 1671 edition of Playford, and only two are carried over from the earlier publication. Three are taken from the group of six hymns first published in the mid-sixteenth century and these are reproduced here.

Example 26.

Humble Suit of a Sinner
John Playford, *The Whole Book of Psalms*, 1677, pp. 283-285.
This Tune or to *Windsor Tune*.

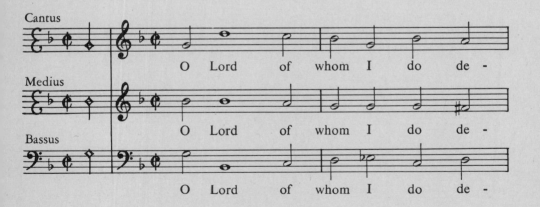

---

[1] John Playford. *The Whole Book of Psalms*, London, 1677, Preface, unpaged.

Example 27.

The Lamentation of a Sinner
John Playford, *The Whole Book of Psalms,* 1677, pp. 285-287.

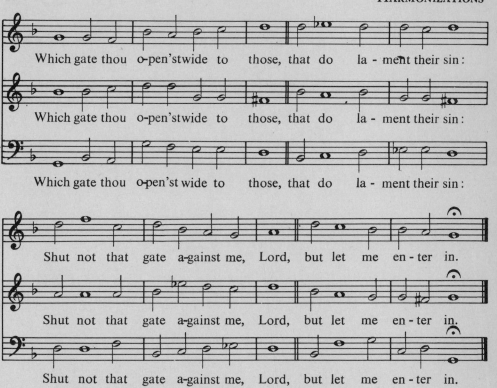

Which gate thou o-pen'st wide to those, that do la - ment their sin:

Which gate thou o-pen'st wide to those, that do la - ment their sin:

Which gate thou o-pen'st wide to those, that do la - ment their sin:

Shut not that gate a-gainst me, Lord, but let me en - ter in.

Shut not that gate a-gainst me, Lord, but let me en - ter in.

Shut not that gate a-gainst me, Lord, but let me en - ter in.

A fourth edition of the Psalter, published in 1698, kept the same hymns from the earliest Sternhold and Hopkins with only a few changes in the music, except for *The Lamentation of a Sinner*. In the 1698 volume the hymn is set to *Martyrs Tune*.

Example 28.

The Lamentation of a Sinner
John Playford, *The Whole Book of Psalms,* 4th ed., 1698, p. 281.
Martyrs Tune

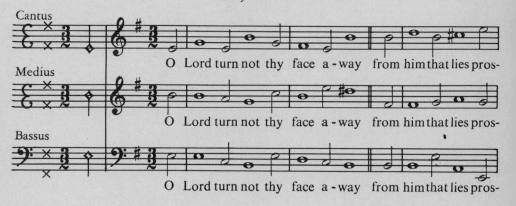

O Lord turn not thy face a - way from him that lies pros-

O Lord turn not thy face a - way from him that lies pros-

O Lord turn not thy face a - way from him that lies pros-

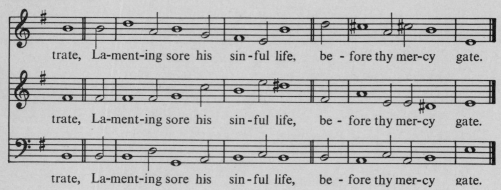

trate, La-ment-ing sore his   sin-ful life,   be - fore thy mer-cy   gate.

trate, La-ment-ing sore his   sin-ful life,   be - fore thy mer-cy   gate.

trate, La-ment-ing sore his   sin-ful life,   be - fore thy mer-cy   gate.

Example 29.

A Penitential Hymn
John Playford, *The Whole Book of Psalms*, 1677, pp. 287-288.
Proper Tune

Cantus

O   Lord   in   thee   is   all   my   trust,

Medius

O   Lord   in   thee   is   all   my   trust,

Bassus

O   Lord   in   thee   is   all ___ my   trust,

give   ear   un - to   my   wo - ful   cry:

give   ear   un - to   my   wo - ful   cry:

give   ear   un - to   my   wo - ful   cry:

Re-fuse me not that am un-just, but cast on me thy 'heav'n-ly eye,

Re-fuse me not that am un - just, but cast on me thy heav'n-ly eye,

Re-fuse me not that am un - just, but cast on me thy heav'n-ly eye,

Be-hold how I do still la-ment my sins where-in I do of-fend.

Be-hold how I do still la-ment my sins where-in I do of-fend.

Be-hold how I do still la-ment my sins where-in I do of-fend.

O Lord for them shall I be shent, sith thee to please I do in-tend?

O Lord for them shall I be shent, sith thee to please I do in-tend?

O Lord for them shall I be shent, sith thee to please I do in-tend?

These harmonizations by Playford reveal a chordal approach to the part writing and yet the modal quality is not entirely abandoned, for he still alters a note to make a major third in the cadence and immediately uses it unaltered in the following chord. The final chord in the cadence is rarely complete and at the end is without either third or fifth. This last, no doubt, is the result of writing in only three parts but the effect is still not quite that of tonality. Two cross-relations are used in succession in the next to the last bar of the *Martyrs Tune*, Example 28. This kind of insistence on cross-relations, "especially in cadences, represents an attempt to unite modal and tonal concepts."[1]

The medius, while it leaps frequently, seems to be controlled by the other parts rather than having sure direction of its own. Both cantus and medius parts reach higher notes than were found in the highest part of the earlier harmonizations. In the sixteenth-century writing, E-flat was reached only occasionally. Here the parts go up to F.

Root-position chords predominate and the first inversion is less used than in the harmonizations in Este and Ravenscroft.

The long notes at the beginning and end of nearly every phrase tend to become monotonous but Playford was not responsible for this lack of rhythmic variety. In an effort to restore congregational singing to the level it had reached before the Commonwealth, he took the tunes that had been familiar to the people, in the form in which they were usually sung. The music is never weak nor sentimental. It is dignified, though uninspired, and Playford's contribution to the advancement of congregational singing should not be underestimated.

The last important Psalter published before the advent of Isaac Watts' hymnals was *A new Version of the Psalms of David fitted to the tunes used in Churches* brought out in 1696 by Nahum Tate (1652-1715), Irish poet laureate, and Dr. Nicholas Brady (1659-1726). This first edition did not include any hymns, but *A Supplement To The New Version of Psalms, By Dr. Brady and Mr. Tate, Containing, The Psalms in Particular Measure; the usual Hymns . . . and Tunes (Treble and Bass) proper to each of them, and all the rest of the Psalms* was accorded royal authority in 1703. Here among the hymns, which included "While shepherds watched their flocks by night," was the old *Lamentation* hymn with new tune.

---

[1] Manfred F. Bukofzer, *Music in the Baroque Era*, New York, 1947, p. 215.

Example 30.

Lamentation of a Sinner
N. Tate and N. Brady, *A Supplement to the New Version of Psalms,*
10th ed., 1703, p. 133.
Ten Commandments Tune

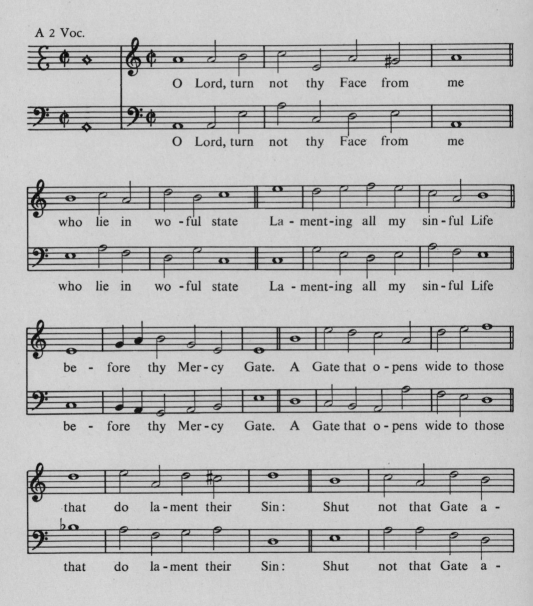

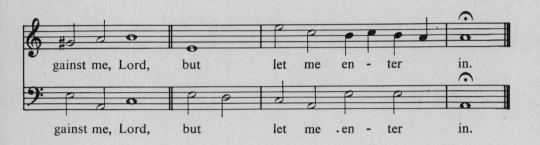

gainst me, Lord,   but   let   me   en - ter   in.

gainst me, Lord,   but   let   me .en - ter   in.

[In the last system, the third bass note, printed C in the Psalter, should probably be E.]

This "new" tune continues the practice which had been established at the end of the Commonwealth of starting and closing each phrase with a long note. Within the phrase, the notes are generally the same length but there are indications of a trend away from syllabic settings using half-notes. The major/minor tonality is well established. The cadence of the fourth phrase, with the words "Mercy Gate," is unusual. The seventh above the A is not as unexpected as the fourth above the B. One wonders if there has been a misprint. The whole phrase has a folk-tune quality. The sixth and octave leaps which we find in the tune are radical departures from the size of leaps used in the previous tunes and would distinguish it as a "new" tune even if it were not so marked in the Psalter.

Thus we come to the end of the era of Psalm Books. Playford's Psalter continued in print until the last part of the eighteenth century, the twentieth edition coming out in 1757. Sternhold and Hopkins was used until the nineteenth century; Tate and Brady until the late nineteenth century.

As the course of these six hymn tunes has been followed through nearly 150 years of publication, it has been seen that the changes in musical practices of the periods in which the various harmonizations were made are reflected in the compositions, even though the pieces are of very small proportions. In the early tunes which are not harmonized, and for which no composers are known, the rhythmic pattern which was produced by following the accents and flow of the words is the outstanding characteristic. It seems to be in imitation of the Gregorian music, which was discarded with the severance from Roman ties, only in this easy flow of the rhythm. Melodically, the range is wider, and the mystic quality of the Gregorian is replaced by a straightforward, plain but sincere religious feeling. The first harmonizations, dating from the late sixteenth century, are contrapuntally conceived with the chords which result from the simultaneous sounding of notes of the various lines showing richness in variety: a characteristic of modal writing. The controlled and careful use of dissonance also is characteristic of the period; the occasional use of some voice leading which was frowned on by the academicians foreshadowing the less strict writing of a later period.

As soon as bar lines became a necessity, and the regular rhythmic pattern set up, apart from the one derived from the text, the tunes lose their freedom and natural expression, even when harmonized by the most skillful madrigal composers. The "tyranny of the bar line" begins in the examples shown from the Este Psalter, and the practice becomes even more objectionable by 1621 when Ravenscroft's Psalter was published. The music in this Psalter is rather pedestrian and even here, in these small pieces, may be seen the beginning of the decline in artistic achievement which takes place in all English music in the last part of the seventeenth century.

The tunes by Playford show Baroque characteristics in an uninspired way. The cross-relations are there, closely spaced. The soprano and the bass are the important parts and the music is built on a strictly chordal basis with the major/minor tonality nearly completely established.

A change in sonority and color was evident in all of the arts during the sixteenth century. The bright colors of the fifteenth century were darkened. The bass part of the music became more important and emphasized. Double basses were in existence by the sixteenth century. The hymn tunes and harmonizations reflect in their own small way this same feeling of depth and darkness which was the result, it has been suggested, of the psychological effects of the environment and strong inhibitions of the people.[1] The tunes throughout the sixteenth century when printed without harmony always appear on a staff with tenor or alto clef. The range is low. In the harmonizations, the tune is always placed in the tenor.

The atmosphere of the eighteenth century was again that of gaiety and light. The transition back to it was made during the seventeenth century. Again the gradual change is reflected in the hymns. The main melodic line is now placed in the highest part. The high notes of the Playford "new tunes" and the "new" tunes in Tate and Brady move easily and frequently up to F, F-sharp, and even G.

It must not be thought that the six hymns discussed here were the only hymns used between 1560 and the beginning of the eighteenth century. There were hundreds of others written, published, and sung during that period. The six were chosen for the study only because they were the first to be used in the service of the English church at the time of the Reformation.

[1] Idea expressed by Curt Sachs at a lecture at Boston University, August, 1956.

The Controversy
about Hymn Singing

Lozd of whō I do depend be holde,

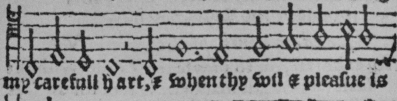

my carefull hart, & when thy wil & pleasue is

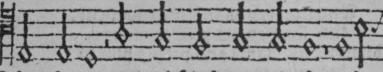

relese me of my smart, thou seest my sozowes

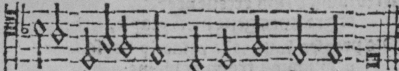

what they ar, my grief is known to the, & there

is non ỹ cā remoue, oz take the same frō me.

But only thou whose ayde I craue,
    whose mercy still is prest
To ease all those that come to thee,
    foz succour and foz rest.
And sith thou seest my restles eyes,
    my teares and greuous grone,
Attende vnto my sute (O Lozde)
    marke well my plaint and mone.
Foz sinne hath so inclosed me
    and compass me aboute:

That

From *The Residue of all Dauids Psalmes,* John Hopkins and others (1562)

CHAPTER IV

T HAS BEEN a long–held belief that freely composed hymns were not an accepted part of the service of the Church of England or of the nonconformist churches until the time of Isaac Watts, whose first hymnal is dated 1707. Over and over one reads in the books that trace the development of the English hymn that no place was given in the church service of the sixteenth and seventeenth centuries for original compositions in English with non-Biblical texts, and that only Psalms were authorized to be sung by the congregation.

That the practice of hymn singing was a controversial subject is evident from the references made to it during the Reformation and later, in sermons, pamphlets, and the like. The very fact that royal permission was necessary and given by the Queen in 1559 shows that hymn singing was not casually accepted. It is not surprising that such was the case. The refugees, coming back to England from Geneva thoroughly imbued with the beliefs of Calvin, wished to become Psalm-singing congregations. Moreover, it was probably true then, as it is now, that in cathedrals and places where the trained choirs sang, there was not a great deal of interest among the music masters in fostering congregational singing. These two forces created enough opposition to or apathy toward hymns so that the impression of no hymn singing was created.

The belief was perpetuated through various channels. Music historians turn their attention, of course, to Services and anthems when studying English church music, searching out those which were written by outstanding composers. If the production of Psalters is mentioned, the books are pictured as being made up entirely of Psalms. We are told that the Pilgrims brought with them to America the Ainsworth Psalter, published without hymns in Holland for the English "Separatists," and yet examination of a 1599 Bible which came with the Pilgrims to Plymouth on the *Mayflower* reveals a Sternhold and Hopkins Psalter bound with it, a Sternhold which included the six hymns discussed in the preceding chapters.

The Old Cheque-Book or Book of Remembrance of the Chapel Royal describes the order of service for the Coronation of Charles in 1625 and there were only anthems sung. Other services outlined used only anthems before and after the sermon.

The often-quoted passage from Mace's *Musick's Monument* relating the siege of the city of York for eleven weeks in 1644, tells of the custom "which I hear not of in any other Cathedral" of singing by the whole congregation of a Psalm before the sermon. This account is used to prove how rare congregational singing was and how it consisted of Psalms.

A Short Direction for the Performance of Cathedrall Service published in 1661 explained that the service was being restored, so the "Ordinary and Extraordinary" parts for priest and choir were given, as well as three tunes in black notes for four parts. The tunes, it was explained, were easily played on the organ "to the quire," if there were anyone who could "prick out the upper and lower parts," but they were to serve only until "Quires were more learnedly Musicall." Another indication that congregations were not expected to participate actively in the service!

In 1789 Burney was still saying "But why is the *whole* congregation to *sing* any more than preach, or read the prayers?"[1]

And as late as 1888 the controversy was being waged by a clergyman of the Church of England who lamented the musical service done en-

---

[1] Burney, *op. cit.*, p. 64.

tirely by choir, saying it was unscriptural, unreal, selfish, sensuous, worldly, uncongregational, and unprotestant.[1]

But what evidence is there that hymns were used? First of all there is their continuous publication beginning c. 1559. Except during the Commonwealth, there were always hymns being published and intended for use in either the Anglican or the nonconformist church from that day to the present time. The first six are found over and over again in succeeding Sternhold Psalters. A 1793 edition examined showed three of the six original ones still surviving. The Psalter of Richard Cotes, 1643, included all six. The Playford Psalters reprinted them. *The Psalms and Hymns usually sung in the Churches and Tabernacles of St. Martin's in the Fields, and St. James's Westminster*, 1688, gave the *Lamentation of a Sinner* with heading *Lords Day the Sixth. Even.* In the table of Psalms and Hymns appropriate for special days, we find the *Lamentation* proper for Good Friday in the morning and for January 30, also at morning service. The hymn is found in later collections when St. Martin's-in-the-Fields and St. James Westminster published separate books. It is difficult to imagine that these hymns would have continued in print over such a long period if they had not been known and used by the people.

There is adequate proof in the Cause Papers presentation of the case against Melchior Smyth that he was using at least one hymn regularly for congregational singing in Trinity Church, Hull, in 1563 or 1564.

Further proof that these hymns and tunes were known and used is found in an Oxford University Press publication of *Seven Hymn-Tunes by John Dowland*, edited by Edmund H. Fellowes and taken from "contemporary Ms. at Welbeck Abbey by kind permission of Duke of Portland." Canon Fellowes says that the seven tunes were composed for the funeral of Henry Noel, an Elizabethan Courtier. The first, fourth, and fifth hymn tunes of the Dowland pieces are the traditional melodies of "O Lord, turn not away thy face," "O Lord, of whom I do depend," and "Where righteousness doth say," and the original words of all three hymns are used either with the music or shown at the end of the music when more modern texts are supplied by Canon Fellowes. Dowland placed the tune in the highest part and provided a four-part harmonization, but Canon Fellowes' inference that John Dowland was the com-

---

[1] *Musical Service Is it Right?*, London, 1888.

poser of the tunes is in error, as they had appeared in print before the birth of Dowland. However, the important fact here is that the composer selected the hymns to use in this way. Today when composers reharmonize hymn tunes or make them into organ preludes, they usually select those which are best known. One would suppose that Dowland also did this. It should be noted, too, that these seven pieces are referred to as Psalms in *Music in the Renaissance*[1] even though only four of them are Psalms.

William Barton (c. 1603-1678) , a conforming Puritan and writer of several Centuries of Select Hymns, all carefully notated with Biblical texts, called the *Complaint of a Sinner* "nonsensical."[2] And in the *Three Last Centuries,* speaking of tunes in the Preface, he says

> Note, That the Tune call'd Where Righteousness, etc. may be changed into the usual Tune of the 67 Psalm if you put in two Sillables more in the third Line of every four.[3]

In 1720 Simon Browne published *Hymns and Spiritual Songs.* As so many editors did, he traces the history of hymn singing in the Preface to his book. His account relates that

> At the Reformation here, or about that time, David's psalms were not only turned into English metre, but it was also thought proper to turn some of these Latin hymns in like manner, such as Te Deum, Veni creator Spiritus, and to add some new ones such as, The humble Suit of a Sinner, The Complaint of a Sinner, The Lamentation etc. which were commonly bound up with the version of the psalms by Sternhold, Hopkins, etc. and used both in publick assemblies and private families from the beginning of the Reformation, or at least from its establishment under Queen Elizabeth.

He listed various versions of the Psalms used in England saying that those by Sir Philip Sidney, James I. Sandys, and Barton were well received, as were hymns by Mr. Mason and Mr. Herbert's poems turned into common meter. All of these hymns and Psalms he knew to be in common use, "either in private families or Christian assemblies till within a few years past."

---

[1] Reese, *op. cit.,* p. 810.

[2] *A Dictionary of Hymnology,* edited by John Julian, London, 1908, revised ed., p. 346.

[3] William Barton, *Six Centuries of Select Hymns,* London, 1683, 4th ed., Preface to *Three Last Centuries.*

Writing about one hundred and twenty years later than Simon
Browne, the Rev. William Cecil warns that we must distinguish between
what singing is done in rich towns where the churches have organs and
well-taught organists, and in the country villages where there are no
organs. Mr. Cecil's *Church Choir A Collection of Psalm and Hymn
Tunes* reminds the reader of the 1559 Injunctions where the Queen
acknowledged a difference between music adapted for Cathedral or
Collegiate Church and parochial churches. He makes a strong plea for
congregational singing of hymns and quotes the judgment of the Ecclesiastical Court in the case of the Rev. Hutchins versus Denziloe and
Loveland, Churchwardens.[1] The minister prosecuted the churchwardens because they tried to prohibit congregational singing. Judgment by the Right Hon. Sir William Scott was against the authority of
churchwardens in such matters:

> It became the distinguishing mark of the Church, as reformed from
> Popery, to use plain music in opposition to the complex service of the
> Catholics. To perform (hymns) by a select band, with complex music
> very artificially applied . . . is a practice not more reconcileable to
> good taste than to edification; but to sing with plain congregational
> music, is a practice fully authorized.

Because most of the cathedral services did not encourage congregational singing of hymns in the sixteenth century, we should not assume
that the same was true in parish churches. Because of indiscriminate use
of the word Psalm in referring to all poetry within the covers of the
Psalters, we should not assume that the hymns which were also there,
were never used. Because there were only six in the Psalters, we should
not assume that there were no other hymns. Information about the
other hymns does not belong in this book designed to present only the
first six, but a long list could be compiled of hymns by John Austin,
Richard Baxter (and he *did* intend his to be sung), Thomas Campion,
Richard Crashaw, Samuel Crossman, John Donne, Thomas Flatman,
George Herbert, William Hunnis, Benjamin Keach, Thomas Ken, John
Mason, Thomas Shepherd, Joseph Stennett, Jeremy Taylor, Faithfull
Teate, Henry Vaughan, and George Wither. Before 1707 there were
over 500 hymns by these poets printed in books and intended to be

---

[1] See Haggard's Reports of the Consistory Court, Vol. 1.

sung; 115 more before 1755. Because there was no leader in the English Reformation with the musical understanding and discrimination of Martin Luther to guide and nurture hymn singing, we should not assume that it could not develop. Why would those opposed to hymn singing have been continually on the defensive about it if they had been successful in stopping its use?

Hymn singing is a natural means of expression of prayer and praise to God, and it thrives in spite of opposition and hostility. English hymnody is witness of this fact. It grew from a very small nucleus of hymns which, like the Latin office hymns, had a pseudo-liturgical significance. The hymns may have "elbowed" their way into the service and battled to stay there but they have been present ever since the mid-sixteenth century.

APPENDIX

HERE IS SOME question about the colophon date 1569 being correct for the Sternhold and Hopkins Psalter called "the first parte." A description of the volume and of the Hopkins Psalter called "The Residue" used in this study follows, along with discussion of the evidence found which makes the date 1569 for the Sternhold seem spurious.

Title page of the Sternhold and Hopkins Psalter with questionable date of 1569:

The first parte/ of the Booke of Psalmes, col-/lected into English Metre, by/ Thomas Sternehold, Jhon Hopkins/and others: conferred with the/ Hebrue, with apte notes to singe/ them withall./

Newly set forth and allowed to be song/ in Churches, of al the people together,/ before and after Mornyng and Euening Prayer, as also before and after the Ser-/mons and moreouer in priuate houses, for their/ godly solace and comfort, laying apart all un-/godly songes and balades, which tende/ onely to the nourishyng of vice, and corrupting of youth./ Wherunto is added the Catechisme for chil-/dren, and also a short introduction to/ learne to sing these Psalmes./ James. 5./ If any be afflicted, let him pray, and if any/ be mery, let him sing Psalmes./ Collos. 3./ Let the worde of God dwel plenteouslye in all/ wisdom, teaching and exhorting one an other in Psalmes, Hymnes, and spiritual

97

songes,/ and sing unto the Lord in your harts./ Imprinted at London
by Jhon Daye./ Cum priuilegio Regie Maiestatis/per Decennium./
Forbidding all other to printe these/ Psalmes or any part of them.

Colophon

Imprinted at London by John Daye, dwelling ouer Aldergate, Anno.
1569 Cum gratia & priuilegio Regiae Maiestatis per decenium. These
bookes of Psalmes are to be sold at his shop under the gate.

Contents

A Catechisme
A Short introduction into the science of Musike
Veni creator [with tune]
Venite exultemus
Te Deum [with tune]
Benedictus [with tune]
Magnificat [with tune]
Nunc Dimittis [with tune]
Quincunque vult [with tune]
The Lamentation of a sinner [with tune]
The Lordes prayer [with tune]
The X Commandments [with tune]

Psalmes

    1-34, 37, 41-44, 49-52, 62-75, 78, 79, 82, 100, 103,
       114, 115, 119-121, 123-125, 127-130, 133, 137,
       146, 148, 117, 134.
       Tunes with 1, 3, 6, 14, 18, 21, 25, 30, 41, 44,
       50, 51, 52, 68, 69, 72, 78, 100, 103, 119, 120,
       121, 124, 125, 127, 130, 137, 148. [Twenty-eight
       tunes in this section.]

The X Commandments [with tune]
A prayer
The Lordes prayer
Articles of the Christian Faith [with tune]
A prayer vnto the holy ghost, to be song before the Sermon
Da pacem domine [with tune]
The complaint of a sinner [with tune]
A thankesgeuing after the receiuing of the Lordes supper
Preserves us Lorde by thy dear word
Through perfect repentaunce the sinner hath a sure trust in
      God that his sinnes shalbe washed away in Christes
      bloud.   [With tune]   [A Lamentation]

FINIS

A forme of prayer to be vsed in priuate houses, every mornying
    and euenyng
The Letany
Prayers
A Table both for the number of the Psalmes: and also in what
    leafe ye may finde them.

[Eighty Psalms, five hymns,[1] and five canticles. Forty-two tunes.]

Title page of the Hopkins Psalter of 1562:

*The Residue/ of all Dauids Psalmes in metre, made by John Hop-
kins and/ others, with apt notes to syng them/ withal. Faythfully perused and/ alowed according to thordre/ appointed in the Quenes/
maiesties Iniunctios./ Nowe fyrst Imprinted and sette/ forth in this
fourme/ for such as haue bookes alredy, that thei that be disposed/ maye
joyne these wyth them: and so/ to haue the whole Psalmes./ . . .* Imprinted at London by John Daye/ dwellyng ouer Aldersgate./ Cum
gratia & priuilegio Regie Maiesta-/tis, per septennium./ 1562.

Contents

Psalmes
       35, 36, 38-40, 45-48, 50, 51, 53-61, 76, 77, 80, 81,
       83-102, 104-113, 116-118, 122, 125, 126, 131, 132, 134-
       136, 138-145, 147, 149, 150.
       Tunes with 35, 46, 50, 59, 61, 77, 81, 88, 95, 104, 111,
       113, 122, 125, 132, 134, 135, 136, 141, 145, 147.
       [Twenty-two tunes in this section.]
The Humble Sute of the Sinner [with tune]
The Song of 3 Children [with tune]

[Seventy-six Psalms, one hymn, and one canticle. Twenty-four tunes.]

Examination shows that a complete Psalter[2] was indeed provided
if the Hopkins "Residue" and the Sternhold and Hopkins "first parte"
were used together. These two volumes also provided all the expected
hymns, canticles, prayers, creed, etc. Examination of the 1556, 1558,

[1] Five hymns with poetry written originally in English, three Latin hymns translated into
English, and one German hymn translated into English.
[2] Psalms 50, 51, 100, 117, 125, and 134 are in both books. In Sternhold and Hopkins, Psalms
50 and 51 are by W. Whit.; 100 by Hopkins; 117 and 134 by T. B. [econ]; 125 by Wisdome. In
Hopkins, Psalm 50 is by Hopkins; 51 and 117 by Norton; 100 by Hopkins; 125 and 134 by Kethe.

1560, 1561 (Genevan and English) editions of Sternhold and Hopkins shows that none of these other volumes published before the Hopkins "Residue" completes it.

Another copy of the "first parte" of the Psalms dated 1564, S. T. C. 2433, is in the Henry E. Huntington Library. A microfilm of it shows that the title page is unlike that of the Boston copy. John Hopkins is not mentioned by name, the authors being given as Thomas Sternholde and others. Where the Boston copy says "Newly set forth etc., the Huntington copy reads "faythfully perused and allowed, according to thordre appoynted in the Queenes maiestyes Iniunctions." There is no mention of singing in churches. The Huntington copy was printed with privilege for seven years. Both volumes include the "Cathechism" and also a "Short Introduction to Learn to Syng the Psalms." The texts and tunes of the two books are the same and, with only a few exceptions, are printed on pages which correspond in number. In the Catechism, next to last page, the Huntington copy reads "To honour and obey the king and his ministers." The Boston copy reads "To honour and obey ye Queene, and her ministers." Psalm CXV in the Huntington copy is accompanied with a tune and the text begins

> Not unto us (O Lord)
> I say to us giue none:
> But geue al prayse of grace and truth
> unto thy name alone.

In the Boston copy there are instructions to sing the Psalm as Psalm 78 and the text begins

> Not unto us Lord, not to us,
> but to thy name geue praise:
> Both for the mercy and the truth,
> that are in thee alwayes.

Both editions have eighteen stanzas for this Psalm but because of the different versions the placing of the following Psalms does not come on pages with corresponding numbers in the two books, as had been the procedure up to this place. By Psalm CXX they are proceeding together again. There is a difference in tunes given for Psalm CXX in the two books. The tune shown in the Boston copy has bar lines in it, which is most unusual for either book. There are various differences in spelling and punctuation throughout the volumes.

A comparison of the first complete Sternhold and Hopkins Psalter in one volume published in 1562 with the "first parte" and the Hopkins "Residue" shows these differences:

first parte	Residue	Complete
Ps. 19 by J.H.		Ps. 19 by T. S. (but text the same as "first parte")
Ps. 31 by T. S.		Ps. 31 by J. H.
	Ps. 38 by Norton	Ps. 38 by J. H.
Ps. 51 by W.Whit.	Ps. 51 by Norton	Ps. 51 by W. Whit. and another by Norton
	Ps. 77 has no tune	Ps. 77 with tune
Ps. 100 by J. H.	Ps. 100 by J. H.	Ps. 100 Anon. (but text the same as "Residue")
	Ps. 102 by Norton	Ps. 102 by J. H.
	Ps. 111 by Kethe	Ps. 111 by Norton
	Ps. 112 has no tune	Ps. 112 has tune
Ps. 125 by Wisdome	Ps. 125 by Kethe	Ps. 125 by Kethe

The copy of the "first parte," now at the Boston Public Library, was formerly in the library of Lord Aldenham, and attached to the back cover is page seventy-one of a book dealer's catalogue [Ellis and Elvey, 1896]. It reads as follows:

29 New Bond Street
Elizabethan Church Service

540 Psalter (The,/ . . . 1569. The Psalter,/ . . . 1570. . . . The/ Epistles and Gospels./ . . . 1569. The first parte/ of the Booke of Psalmes, col/ lected into English metre, by/ Thomas Sternehold, Jhon Hopkins/ and others . . . Imprinted at London by Jhon Daye. (n.d.) (Sigs A-S in eights.) [The n.d. is deleted by hand and a notation in the margin states:] 1569 misprint for 1559 see my catalogue Supplt. p. 19.

The Residue of all Davids Psalmes in metre, made by John Hopkins and others, etc. . . . . . Imprinted at London by John Daye. 1562. (Sigs A-N4 in eights) 5 parts in 1 vol., thick 8vo. Black letter, in the original calf binding of the period, the sides and back richly gilt and coloured, gauffre edges. A most beautiful example of ornamental binding of the XVIth century in perfect preservation, in a morocco case.

A most remarkable collection of early and rare Elizabethan editions of the Psalter & c., all of which are in perfect condition. The freshness of the contemporary binding of this volume is extraordinary. See frontispiece to this Catalogue.

Handwritten in ink on the flyleaf of the book is the notation: "Aldenham 1896," and in pencil: "Bought of Ellis £100."

The *Catalogue of the Aldenham Library*, First Portion, sold on March 24, 1937 by Messrs. Sotheby and Company, gives this description of the same volume:

Extremely rare. In fine Condition. Bound in 1 vol. in a very fine contemporary English Binding; brown calf, elaborate centre and corner-pieces with arabesque and foliate designs stamped in relief on azured grounds; a part of the ground surrounding the centre-piece decorated with a semis of small conventional flowers; traces of colour (red, green and white) remain; back decorated by three horizontal bands composed of two small rectangular compartments and two oval within gold lines separated by two bands and arabesque ornament; edges and back tooled au pointillé. In a morocco case; sold as a collection and not subject to return. Bought of Ellis in 1896.

I have been unable to locate the catalogue supplement referred to in the handwritten notation on the margin of the Ellis catalogue quoted above, but if the 1559 date is correct, the book could have been the intended partner for the Hopkins "Residue" of 1562.

John Day did publish some Psalms in 1559. Steele says that Day profited more than any other printer from the Injunctions of Elizabeth sanctioning the use of hymns or such like songs. Mention is made of him in the original charter of the Stationers' Company in 1556, but he did not take up the Livery until 1561. An entry in the Stationers' Registers (i 124) has not yet been satisfactorily explained:

Receyued of John Daye for a fyne for printinge of serten copyes without lysense and contrary to the orders of this howse, *a quatron of psalmes with notes* the ijde of octobre. (1559) [1]

---

[1] Robert Steele, *Earliest English Music Printing*, London, 1903, p. 11.

Reference to this same 1559 edition of the Psalms with tunes is found in the Introduction to the Historical Edition of *Hymns Ancient and Modern*.[1] The printing of the book was in some way irregular and, we are told, no copy of it is known nor is it clear whether it was ever issued.

The Hopkins Psalter is perhaps a unique copy. An article by F.G.E. in the November, 1907, issue of the *Musical Times,* has this interesting account of it:

> The Residue of all David's Psalmes sold by Messrs. Puttick and Simpson on Dec. 3, 1872. Bound up with other liturgical books. Lot 508.
>
> "Herbert informs us that toward the end of the year 1561, Day had license to print 'the resydewe of the Psalmes not heretofore prynted, so that this maketh up the hole.' But he had evidently never seen a copy of the printed volume."

The book was sold for 101 pounds. Dr. Arber's transcript of the Registers of the Company of Stationers of London is quoted. Here is given the terms of the license to John Day to print the book under date July, 1561, to July, 1562. "Recevyd of John Daye for his lycense for pryntinge of the Resydewe of the psalmes not here to fore printed. So that this maketh vp the hole iiij d."

Perhaps someone will be able to help date the Boston copy of the "first parte." The privilege of printing for ten years indicates that the 1569 date is correct, but the Huntington "first parte" (1564) shows the privilege for seven years. Could the Boston copy be a re-issue of an earlier edition? Or if the date of the Boston volume should prove to be 1559, could the book have been published so early in the year that it came before the royal permission for the singing of hymns and for this reason the publisher was fined?

[1] P. xliii

Chronological List of
Psalters Used in This Study

Sternhold, Thomas. *Certayne Psalmes chose out of the Psalter of David, and drawe into Englishe Metre.* Londini: Edouardus Whitchurche, 1547. Microfilm. British Museum, G 12147. S.T.C. 2419.

Crowley, Robert. *The Psalter of David newely translated into Englyshe metre in such sort that it maye the more decently, and wyth more delyte of the mynde be reade and songe of al men. Wherunto is added a not of four partes.* Eley rentes in Holburne: Robert Crowley, 1549.

Sternhold, Thomas. *Alsuch Psalmes of David, as Thomas Sternhold, late Grome of the kinges maiesties robes did in his lyfe time drawe into English metre.* 1549. Microfilm. British Museum, G 12148. S.T.C. 2421.

Seagar, Francis. *Certayne Psalmes select out of the Psalter of David, and drawn into Englyshe Meter, with Notes to every Psalm in iiij parts to Synge.* London: wyllyam Seres, 1553.

Sterneholde, Thomas, and others. *Psalmes of David in Englishe Metre by Thomas Sterneholde and others: conferred with the Ebrue, and in certein places corrected, as the sense of the Prophet required: and, in this second edition are added eleuen mo, newly composed.* 1558. [This is the Anglo-Genevan Psalter and part of *The Forme of Prayers and Ministration of the Sacraments, . . . used in the Englishe Congregation at Geneua: and approued, by . . . Iohn Caluin.* Printed at Geneva by James Poullain and Antoine Rebul. 1558.] Microfilm. Henry E. Huntington Library. S.T.C. 16561a.

Certaine notes set forth in foure and three parts to be song at the Morning Communion, and euening praier . . . Imprinted at London . . . by John Day, 1560. Medius and Bassus parts. British Museum, K.7.e.7.

Sterneholde, Thomas, and others. *Psalmes of David in Englishe Metre, by Thomas Sterneholde and others: conferred with the Hebrue, and in certeine places corrected, as the sense of the Prophete required: and the Note joyned withall. Very mete to be vsed of all sorts of people priuatly for their godly solace and confort, laying aparte all vngodly songes & ballades, which tende only to the norishing of vice and corrupting of youth. Newly set fourth and allowed, according to the order appointed in the Quenes Maiesties Iniunctions.* . . . 1560. Microfilm. Christ Church, e.8.6 S.T.C. 2427.

Hopkins, John, and others. *The Residue of all Dauids Psalmes in metre, made by John Hopkins and others, with apt notes to syng them withal. Faythfully perused and alowed according to thordre appointed in the Quenes maiesties Iniunctiōs. Nowe fyrst Imprinted and sette forth in this fourme for such as haue bookes alredy, that thei that be disposed maye joyne these wyth them: and so to haue the whole Psalmes.* . . . London: John Day, 1562. Boston Public Library, Benton 16.01.1.

Starnhold, T., Hopkins, J., and others. *The Whole Booke of Psalmes, collected into Englysh metre by T. Starnhold J. Hopkins &·others: conferred with the Ebrue, with apt Notes to synge the withal, Faithfully perused and alowed according to thordre appointed in the Quenes maiesties Iniunctions. Very mete to be vsed of all sortes of people priuately for their solace and comfort: laying apart all vngodly Songes and Ballades, which tende only to the norishing of vyce, and corrupting of youth.* . . . Lōdon: John Day, 1562.

The whole psalmes in foure partes. Tenor part book. London: John Day, 1563.

Sternholde, Thomas, and others. *The first parte of the Psalmes collected into Englishe Meter, by Thomas Sternholde, and others, conferred wyth the Hebrew, with apte Notes to sing them withal, faythfully perused and allowed, according to thorder appoynted in the Queens maiestyes Iniunctions. Very meete to be used of all sortes of people priuatly for their godly solace and comfort, laying aparte al ungodly songes and balades, whych tend only to the nourishyng of vyce and corruptyng of youth. Wherunto is added the Cathechisme, and also a short introduction to learne to syng the Psalmes.* London: John Day, 1564. Microfilm. Henry E. Huntington Library. S.T.C. 2433.

Mornyng an Euenyng prayer and Communion, set forthe in foure partes to be song in churches, both for men and children . . . wyth dyuers other godly prayers and Anthems, of sundry mens doynges. London: John Day, 1565. Medius, Tenor, Contratenor part books. British Museum, K.7.e.8.

Parker, Matthew. *The Whole Psalter translated into English Metre, which contayneth an hundred and fifty psalmes.* London: John Daye [c. 1567].

Sternehold, Thomas, and Jhon Hopkins, and others. *The first parte of the Booke of Psalmes, collected into English Metre . . . conferred with the Hebreu, with apte notes to singe them withall.* London: Jhon Day, 1569. Boston Public Library, Benton 16.01.1.

Daman, Guilielmo. *The Psalmes of David in English meter, with Notes of foure partes set vnto them, by Guilielmo Daman, for Iohn Bull.* London: John Daye, 1579. Tenor and Bassus part books. British Museum, K.4.C.5. Photostat Treble and Contratenor part books, B.370.y.

Byrd, William. *Psalmes, Sonets, and songs of sadness and pietie, made into musike of five parts.* Thomas East, 1588, Superius part book.

Damon, M. William. *The second Booke of the Musicke of M. William Damon . . . conteining all the tunes of Dauids Psalmes, as they are ordinarily soung in the Church.* T. Este, the assigne of W. Byrd, 1591. British Museum, K.7.a.3.

Allison, Richard. *The Psalmes of Dauid in Meter, The plaine Song beeing the common tunne to be sung and plaide vpon the Lute, Orphatyon, Citterne or Base Violl, seuerally or altogether, the singing part to be either Tenor or Treble to the Instrument . . .* London: William Barley, the Assigne of Thomas Morley, 1599. British Museum, K.7.f.10.

Sternhold, Thomas, and John Hopkins, and others. *The Whole Book of Psalmes.* London: John Windet for the Assignes of Richard Daye, 1599.

——. *The Whole Book of Psalmes.* 1604. Houghton Library. S.T.C. 2517.

The Whole Booke of Psalmes With Their Wonted Tunes, as they are song in Churches, composed into foure parts. 3rd ed. London: Thomas Este, for the companie of Stationers, 1604. Boston Public Library, ** Benton 16.3.

Sternhold, Thomas, and John Hopkins, and others. *The Whole Book of Psalmes.* London: Companie of Stationers, 1616.

——. *The Whole Book of Psalmes.* London: Companie of Stationers, 1619.

Ravenscroft, Thomas. *The Whole Booke of Psalmes with The Hymnes Evangelicall, and Songs Spiritvall. Composed into 4 parts by sundry Authors.* London: Companie of Stationers, 1621. Boston Public Library, Benton 16.5.

Sternhold, Thomas, and John Hopkins, and others. *The Whole Book of Psalmes.* London: Companie of Stationers, 1623.

C. [Cotes], R. [Richard]. *The Whole Booke of David's Psalmes.* London: Company of Stationers, 1643. St. Paul's Cathedral Library, London.

Playford, John. *Psalms and Hymns in Solemn Musick of Foure Parts On the*

Common Tunes to the Psalms in Metre: Used in Parish-Chvrches. London: W. Godbin for J. Playford, 1671.

———. *The Whole Book of Psalms: with The usual Hymns and Spiritual Songs; to-gether with the ancient and proper Tunes sung in Churches* . . . London: W. Godbin for the Company of Stationers, 1677. Houghton Library, Mus. 489.1677.

The Psalms and Hymns Usually sung in the Churches and Tabernacles of St. Martin's in the Fields, and St. James's Westminster. London: R. Everingham for Ric. Chiswell, 1688. British Museum, A.1230.ii.

Tate, Nahum, and Nicholas Brady. *A New Version of the Psalms of David. Fitted to the Tunes Used in Churches.* M. Clark for the Company of Stationers, 1696.

Select Psalms and Hymns for the Use of the Parish Church and Tabernacle of St. James Westminster. Companie of Stationers, 1697. British Museum, 3091. a.13.

Playford, John. *The Whole Book of Psalms with the Usual Hymns and Spiritual Songs.* 4th ed. London: J. Hepinstall for the Companie of Stationers, 1698.

Brady, Nicholas, and Nahum Tate. *A Supplement To The New Version of Psalms.* 10th ed. London: Pearson for R. Ware, 1703.

Browne, Simon. *Hymns and Spiritual Songs by Simon Browne.* London: Printed for Eman Matthews, at the Bible in Pater-Noster-Row, 1720. British Museum, 3436.e.21.

Selected Bibliography

A Short Direction of the Performance of Cathedrall Service: Published for the Information of such Persons, as are Ignorant of it, and shall be call'd to officiate in Cathedrall, or Collegiate Churches, where it hath formerly been in use. Oxford: Hall and Davis, 1661. St. Paul's Cathedral Library, London.

Benson, Louis F. *The English Hymn.* London: Hodder and Stoughton, 1915.

Boyd, Morrison Comegys. *Elizabethan Music and Musical Criticism.* Philadelphia: University of Pennsylvania Press, 1940.

Brawley, Benjamin. *History of the English Hymn.* New York: Abingdon Press, 1932.

Bukofzer, Manfred F. *Music in the Baroque Era.* New York: W. W. Norton Co., 1947.

Burney, Charles. *A General History of Music.* 4 vols. London: Printed for the Author, 1789.

Christophers, S. W. *Hymn Writers and Their Hymns.* London: S. W. Partridge, 1866.

Coverdale, Myles. "Goostly Psalms and Spirituall Songs," in *Remains of Myles Coverdale.* Edited by George Pearson. Cambridge, England: University Press, 1846.

Davey, Henry. *History of English Music.* 2nd ed. London: J. Curwen and Sons, 1921.

Douglas, Winfred. *Church Music in History and Practice.* New York: Charles Scribner's Sons, 1937.

Dowland, John. *Seven Hymn-Tunes.* Edited by Edmund H. Fellowes. Tudor Church Music, Second Series, No. 79 and No. 80. London: Oxford University Press.

Duffield, Samuel W. *English Hymns: Their Authors and History.* 3rd ed. revised and corrected. New York: Funk and Wagnalls, 1888.

Fellowes, Edmund H. (ed.). *The Collected Vocal Works of William Byrd.* Vol. XII, *Psalmes, Sonets and Songs* (1588). London: Stainer and Bell Limited. 1948.

Frere, W. H. (ed.). *Hymns Ancient and Modern.* Historical Edition. Printed for the Proprietors. London: William Clowes and Sons, Limited, 1909.

———. *The English Church in the Reigns of Elizabeth and James I.* Vol. V of *A History of the English Church.* Edited by W. R. W. Stephens. London: Macmillan and Co., Ltd., 1904.

———. (ed.). *Visitation Articles and Injunctions of the Period of the Reformation.* 2 vols. London: Longmans Green and Co., 1915.

Frost, Maurice. *English and Scottish Psalm and Hymn Tunes c. 1543-1677.* London: Oxford University Press, 1953.

Gillman, Frederick John. *The Evolution of the English Hymn.* New York: Macmillan Co., 1935.

Jefferson, H. A. L. *Hymns in Christian Workshop.* New York: Macmillan Co., 1950.

Jordan, W. K. *The Development of Religious Toleration in England.* Vol. I: *From the Beginning of the English Reformation to the Death of Queen Elizabeth.* Cambridge: Harvard University Press, 1932.

Julian, John (ed.). *A Dictionary of Hymnology.* Revised edition with new supplement. London: John Murray, 1907.

Lightwood, James T. *Hymn Tunes and Their Story.* London: Epworth Press, 1923.

Marks, Harvey B. *The Rise and Growth of English Hymnody.* London: Revell Co., 1937.

McCuthan, Robert Guy. *Hymns in the Lives of Men.* New York: Abingdon-Cokesbury Press, 1945.

Miller, Josiah. *Singers and Songs of the Church.* New York: Anson D.F. Randolph Company, 1875.

Morley, Thomas. *A Plain and Easy Introduction to Practical Music.* Edited by R. Alec Harman. New York: W. W. Norton, [1952].

Musical Service, Is It Right? London: James Nesbit Company, 1888.

Patrick, Millar. *Four Centuries of Scottish Psalmody.* London: Oxford University Press, 1949.

Phillips, C. Henry. *The Singing Church.* London: Faber, 1945.

Phillips, C. S. *Hymnody, Past and Present.* New York: Macmillan Co., 1937.

Purvis, J. S. *Tudor Parish Documents of the Diocese of York.* Cambridge University Press, 1948.

Reese, Gustave. *Music in the Renaissance.* New York: W. W. Norton Co., 1954.

Rimbault, Edward F. (ed.). *The Old Cheque-Book or Book of Remembrance of The Chapel Royal* from 1561-1744. Camden Society, 1872.

Routley, Erik. *Hymns and Human Life.* New York: Philosophical Library, 1953.

Selborne, Palmer Roundell, Earl of. *Hymns Their History and Development.* London: Adam and Charles Black, 1892.

Steele, Robert. *The Earliest English Music Printing.* Bibliographical Society at the Chiswick Press, 1903.

Strunk, Oliver (ed.). *Source Readings in Music History.* New York: W. W. Norton Co., 1950.

Walker, Ernest. *A History of Music in England.* 3rd ed. revised by J. A. Westrup. Oxford: Clarendon Press, 1952.

Warton, Thomas. *The History of English Poetry.* London: Alex Murray and Son, 1870.

Wordsworth, Christopher, and Henry Littlehales. *The Old Service Books of the English Church.* London: Methuen Co., 1904.

Articles and Periodicals

Benson, Louis F. "The Liturgical Use of English Hymns." *The Princeton Theological Review*, X (April, 1912) .

Catalogue of the Aldenham Library, Third Day's Sale, by Messrs. Sotheby and Co., Wednesday, March 24, 1937, Lot 304. London: H. Davy.

F.G.E. "The Residue of all David's Psalmes." *Musical Times* (November, 1907), 720.

Foote, Henry. "Bibliography for Hymns." *General Theological Seminary Bulletin*, July, 1952.

Harris, Clement A. "Church Choirs in History." *Music and Letters*, XVII (1936), 210 ff.

Injunctions Given by the Queen's Majesty concerning both the clergy and Laity of this Realm. London, 1559. S.T.C. 10095.

Price, Carl F. "What is a Hymn?" *The Papers of the Hymn Society*, VI. New York: The Hymn Society of America, 1937.

Sedgwick, Daniel. *Catalogue of Scarce Religious Poetry containing a choice collection of original Psalms, Hymns, and Poems*. London: No date. Union Theological Seminary Library.

———. *A Comprehensive Index of Names of Original Authors of Hymns Versifiers of Psalms and Translators from Several Languages*. 2nd ed. London: 1863. Union Theological Seminary Library.

INDEX

113